Lally
The Scut

by

Abbie Spallen

directed by Michael Duke

A Tinderbox Theatre Company and MAC co-production
Downstairs at the MAC, Belfast, 14 April to 2 May 2015

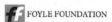

THE MAC

Created at a cost of £18 million, the MAC is Belfast's newest arts venue and houses two theatres, three galleries, dance and rehearsal studios, workshop spaces and an artist-in-residence space as well as offices for resident companies. Our performance spaces allow us to develop unique and exciting collaborations with writers, actors, directors, designers, dancers, musicians and theatre makers that will excite, inspire and entertain audiences from across Northern Ireland and beyond.

Since opening our doors in 2012 with the inaugural MAC production, *Titanic (Scenes from the British Wreck Commissioner's Inquiry, 1912)* by Owen McCafferty, we have welcomed over 750,000 visitors through our doors. Our ambition is to be the leading arts venue in Europe and to foster creativity and innovation amongst home-grown artists as well as those from around the world.

Drawn to our eclectic programme of contemporary art in its many forms, our customers have enjoyed everything from our family Christmas shows (*HATCH!*; *The Incredible Book Eating Boy* and *The Family Hoffmann's Christmas Mystery Palace*, both co-produced with Cahoots NI) to our stunning co-productions with Prime Cut Productions (*God of Carnage; Tejas Verdes; Villa & Discurso; I Am My Own Wife*) and Bruiser Theatre Company (*Cabaret; The 25th Annual Putnam County Spelling Bee* and *Sweet Charity*).

It is entirely fitting therefore that we are continuing our tradition of co-producing by embarking on *Lally the Scut* with our associate artists, Tinderbox, long-term collaborators and friends of the MAC. We are thrilled to be able to help bring this new work to the stage by one of Ireland's finest playwrights, Abbie Spallen.

Under the skilful direction of Michael Duke, we are confident that this huge company of twelve of our finest local actors will deliver this compelling, darkly humorous and ambitious story that will truly resonate with audiences.

To say Northern Ireland theatre is having a moment is how we like to put it! We hope you enjoy the show.

Follow us on:

facebook.com/theMACBelfast

@themacbelfast

instagram.com/themacbelfast

TINDERBOX THEATRE COMPANY

 Tinderbox is Northern Ireland's leading new writing company. For over twenty-five years we have worked with Northern Ireland's most talented playwrights, theatre artists and technicians producing world-class theatre for audiences at home and abroad.

We have premiered over 40 new plays, many of which have earned prestigious new writing and production awards including: the Meyer Whitworth Award, the Stewart Parker Trust Bursary and the Irish Times Best New Play Award.

Tinderbox has established a formidable reputation with a series of landmark productions including the multi-authored and site-specific *Convictions* (2000), **Daragh Carville**'s *Language Roulette* (1996), **Tim Loane**'s *Caught Red Handed* (2002) and *Revenge* by **Michael Duke** (2004). The company has helped to nurture the careers of a generation of writers from Daragh Carville to Stacey Gregg and Owen McCafferty to Abbie Spallen.

Recent successes include **David Ireland**'s *Everything Between Us* (2010) and *Summertime* (2013), **Jimmy McAleavey**'s *The Sign of the Whale* (2010) and *Unhome* (2014), *Planet Belfast* (2012) by **Rosemary Jenkinson** and the site-specific *Guidelines for a Long and Happy Life* by **Paul Kennedy** in 2011.

Tinderbox is a unique theatre company that combines top quality productions, state of the art dramaturgy, versatile outreach projects and special initiatives for Northern Ireland's emerging theatre artists.

Tinderbox is an Associate Artist of the MAC and has presented regularly in the Upstairs theatre since the building opened in 2012. *Lally the Scut* is our first co-production and the first time the company has performed in the main Downstairs theatre.

Artistic Director   Michael Duke
General Manager   Kerry Woods
Dramaturg   Hanna Slättne
Connect Director   Don Mc Camphill

Tinderbox Theatre Company
Imperial Buildings
72 High Street
Belfast
BT1 2BE

T: 028 9043 9313
E: info@tinderbox.org.uk
W: www.tinderbox.org.uk

   @tinderboxNI   facebook.com/tinderboxtheatre

LALLY THE SCUT

Lally the Scut was first performed at the MAC, Belfast,
on Tuesday 14 April 2015 with the following cast

Lally	**Roisin Gallagher**
Ellen	**Carol Moore**
Francis	**Michael Condron**
Rahab	**Maria Connolly**
Owen	**Frank McCusker**
Gavin	**Richard Clements**
Bun McTasney	**Alan McKee**
Daly the Male	**Vincent Higgins**
Digger Barnes	**Gerard McCabe**
Fork the Cat	**Miche Doherty**
Geri Sue	**Tara Lynne O'Neill**
Priest	**Tony Flynn**

PRODUCTION TEAM

Playwright	**Abbie Spallen**
Director	**Michael Duke**
Dramaturg	**Hanna Slättne**
Set & Lighting Designer	**Ciaran Bagnall**
Costume Designer	**Deirdre Dwyer**
Sound Designer	**James Kennedy**
Video Designer	**Conan McIvor**
Voice & Accent Coach	**Peter Ballance**
Production Manager	**Damian Cox**
Deputy Stage Manager	**Noleen Stephenson**
Technical Stage Manager	**Andrew Stanford**
Assistant Stage Manager	**Sarah Gordon**
MAC Technical Team	**Simon Bird, Damian Hughes Gerard McCorry, Chris McCrory**
Producer	**Kerry Woods**
MAC Marketing & PR	**Áine McVerry, Maeve Hawkins and Ciarán Corr**
MAC Operations & FoH	**Lisa McGinley & crew**
Outreach Director	**Don McCamphill**
Outreach Intern	**Naomh Cullen**
Outreach Facilitators	**Finn Kennedy, Patrick Sanders JP Conaghan, Niall Rea**
Design	**AV Browne**
Photography	**Rob Durston**
Set Construction	**Stephen Bamford**

BIOGRAPHIES

Roisin Gallagher | LALLY

Roisin is from Belfast and trained at the Royal Conservatoire of Scotland.

Theatre credits include: *Stitched Up* C21 Theatre Co; *The Holy Holy Bus* Brassneck Theatre Co; *Pentecost, Demented, Weddins, Weeins' and Wakes, White Star of the North, Dockers* and *Be My Baby* Lyric Theatre; *The Trouble with Harry* TheatreofPluck; *Belfast by Moonlight* Kabosh Theatre Co; *A Midsummer Night's Dream* Royal Lyceum Theatre; *The Christening* Rawlife Theatre Co; *Aladdin* Lana Productions; *The Haunting of Helena Blunden* Big Telly Theatre Co; *Sleep Eat Party* Tinderbox Theatre Co; *The Wicked Lady* New Vic; *Cinderella* C21 Theatre Co; *The Bloody Chamber* Northern Stage; *Much Ado About Nothing* and *The Merchant of Venice* Glasgow Rep.

TV credits include: *Doctors* BBC One; *The Fall* BBC Two.

Radio credits include: *Translations* BBC Radio Four; *Ulster Volunteers* RTE Radio One; *Love Letters from the Front* BBC Radio Ulster.

Film credits include: *Made in Belfast* KGB Productions; *To Lose Control* Scattered Images; *Eyeline* Marine Media.

Carol Moore | ELLEN

Theatre credits include: *Pentecost, Can't Forget About You, Macbeth, The Blind Fiddler, Weddins, Weeins and Wakes, Death of a Salesman, Those You Pass on the Street, Belfast by Moonlight, Titans, 1 in 5, Two Roads West, Henry and Harriet* Kabosh; *The Sweetie Bottle* Brassneck; *Shrieking Sisters* Carol Moore and Maggie Cronin; *The Chairs* Tinderbox.

Film credits include: *The Boxer, Reefer and the Model, Rendezvous* Cleanslate, *Scup* Stirling Productions.

Theatre directing credits: *The Liverpool Boat* Red Lead Arts, *The Jury Room* Tinderbox, *Give My Head Peace* Hull Prod, *Women on the Verge of HRT, Getaway, The Factory Girls, The Cavalcaders, 1974 – The End of the Year Show* Lyric.

Film directing credits: *Pumpgirl* Holywood Productions; *Gort na gCnámh* Straightforward, *This Belfast Thing, Crack the Pavement, History Unfinished, The Farther, The Dearer* and *History Unfinished* NESTA, *The Nuala McKeever Show* UTV.

Awards: 2014 / Support for the Individual Artist (ACNI); 2008 / NI Regional winner BAFTA 60 SEC (History Unfinished); 1988 / Best First Time Director (The Celtic and Foyle Film Festivals).

Michael Condron | FRANCIS

Theatre credits include: *Macbeth, Much Ado About Nothing, John Bull's Other Island, A Very Weird Manor, Xmas Eve Can Kill You, Forget Turkey 1 & 2, The Miser* Lyric Theatre; *Mirandolina* Manchester Royal Exchange; *Mojo-Mickybo* Lyric Hammersmith; *Borderland* 7:84 Theatre Company; *Da* Art NI; *Revenge, The Sign of the Whale* Tinderbox; *The Interrogation of Ambrose Fogarty* GBL Productions; *Oh What A Lovely War, Threepenny Opera, Blue Remembered Hills, The Government Inspector* Bruiser Theatre.

TV and film credits: *Number 2s* BBC; *Last Man Hanging* BBC NI; *Fairytales* BBC; *The Tudors* HBO and *Keith Lemon The Film* Generator Films. Michael has been an integral part of the The Boat Factory since its earliest stages of development and has recently joined the cast for *Game of Thrones*.

Maria Connolly | RAHAB

Maria, from Belfast, trained at the Central School of Speech and Drama, graduating in 1994.

Theatre credits include: *This Other City, Language Roulette, Convictions* Tinderbox; *Two Sore Legs* Green Shoot; *Forget Turkey, Howl, John Bull's Other Island, Macbeth* Lyric; *Belfast By Moonlight, Inventors, Collecting Cultures* Kabosh; *Meeting at Menin Gate, Dancing Shoes* GBL Productions; *That Woman at Rathard* Centre Stage; *The Official Version* Dubbeljoint; *Flaming Fables, The Millies* Replay Productions; *Arden of Faversham* Royal Scottish Academy; *Scenes From the Big Picture, Shopping and F***ing, Problem Child* (nominated for an Irish Times/ESB Best Actress award), *Criminal Genius* Prime Cut Productions; *Hey, Hey Good Looking* Soho Theatre Company; *Energy* Derry Playhouse; *The Pearl* Battersea Arts Centre; *Translations* New Vic; *Silverface* Gate Theatre, Notting Hill; *War of the Roses, Yerma* Embassy Theatre.

Film and television credits include: *Line of Duty* BBC2 World Productions; *Our Robot Overlords* Pinewood Studios; *Ainsprid* TG4; *Survivors* Ulysses Productions; *Betrayal of Trust, The Brendan Smyth Story* BBC NI; *Maru* TG4; *Mickybo and Me* Mickybo Films Ltd; *On Dangerous Ground* Carousel; *A Rap at The Door, Out of The Deep Pan, Made in Heaven* BBC 2.

Writing credits include: *Mabel* Kabosh (currently under commission); *The Chase* Cahoots NI; *Bruised, Massive* Tinderbox; *Bathtime, All Fall Down* Replay; *We Got Tonight* BBC Radio 4 .

Frank McCusker | OWEN

Theatre credits include: *Richard II, The Picture of Dorian Gray, Romeo and Juliet, Julius Caesar, As the Beast Sleeps, The Sanctuary Lamp, Translations, The House, The Tempest, As the Beast Sleeps, The Importance of Being Earnest, She Stoops to Folly* Abbey Theatre; *The Ugly One* Royal Court; *Coriolanus* Globe Theatre; *The Lonesome West* Lyric Theatre, Belfast; *Shadow of a Gunman* Tricycle Theatre; *Defender of the Faith, The Wild Duck, Communion, Shay Mouse* Peacock/Abbey Theatre; *Aristocrats* Lincoln Centre Fest, New York; *Life Support* directed by Harold Pinter, Aldwych Theatre; *The Collection* playing opposite Harold Pinter, Gate Theatre.

Film credits include: *Hunger* Warp Films Ltd; *In Like Flynn* Subotica Films; *The Blackwater Lightship* Hallmark/ Lakeshore; *Inside I'm Dancing* Carrickmore Productions; *The Affair of the Necklace* Warner Bros; *David Copperfield* Hallmark Productions.

TV credits include: *The Fall* Artists Studio; *Titanic* DAP Italy; *Tudors* Showtime; *Bad Girls* Shed Productions; *Murder Prevention* World Productions; *Recoil* Zanzibar/RTE; *Proof* Subotica/RTE; *Pulling Moves* BBC NI.

Richard Clements | GAVIN

Richard trained at Royal Welsh College.

Theatre credits include: *Summertime, Bruised, Caught Red Handed* Tinderbox; *Pride and Prejudice the Musical, Cinderella, The Miser, Observe the Sons of Ulster, Paradise, The Wizard of Oz, The Nativity, What the Reindeer Saw* Lyric Theatre; *Pentecost, Spokesong* Rough Magic/Lyric; *Transparency* Ransom; *Arguments for Terrorism* (Oran Mor/Ransom; *Titanic Boys* GBL; *Collecting Culture* Kabosh; *The Old Curiosity Shop* Gate Theatre; *Over the Bridge* Green Shoot; *Confusions, Blue Remembered Hills, Oh What a Lovely War* Bruiser;

Stitched Up, Zoo Story, Time Flies C21; *Same Time Next Year* Skewiff/Belfast Film Festival; *Comedy of Errors* Theatre at the Mill; *Have a Nice Life* Pleasance; *Lovers* Big Telly; *The Dreamer Examines His Pillow* Stray Dawg; *Danny Boy* Westcliff Palace.

Film and TV credits include: *The Frankenstein Chronicles; Good Vibrations; The Keith Lemon Movie; Free Spirits; Titanic Town; S.O.S The Titanic Inquiry; Betrayal of Trust; Scapegoat; At Water's Edge; Wodehouse in Exile; The English Class; I Can't Stop My Dream* NI Screen Short; *Cleansed* NI Screen Short / Belfast Film Festival 2015; *A Christmas Star* due for release in November 2015 and the second season of *The Fall.*

Richard also worked at the Traverse Theatre at last years Edinburgh Festival on *Spoiling* which won a Fringe First award and transferred to the Theatre Royal in Stratford East.

Alan McKee | BUN McTASNEY

Previous Tinderbox productions include *Can't Pay, Won't Pay, Language Roulette, Convictions, Caught Red Handed* and *The Duke of Hope* (co-writer with Conor Grimes).

Other theatre credits include: *The History of the Troubles ... Accordin' to My Da, Bah Humbug, The Nativity, What the Donkey Saw, Over the Bridge, National Anthem, Paradise: the Belfast Celtic Story, Observe the Sons of Ulster Marching Towards the Somme, Metamorphosis, A Love Song for Ulster* and *Saint Mungo's Luganulk.*

Film/TV/radio credits include: *The Craic, Divorcing Jack, Everybody's Gone, The Truth Commissioner, The Tractor Show, The Visitors, Motormouth, Eureka Street, Two Doors Down.*

Alan is an associate artist with the Global Arts Corps and a member of the Northern Ireland Equity Committee.

Vincent Higgins | DALY THE MALE

Vincent is an actor and writer from Co Antrim.

Theatre credits include: *Convictions* Tinderbox; *Those You Pass on the Street, Inventors, 1 in 5, Titans, Carnival, Two Roads West* Kabosh; *The Septic Tiger* Rawlife; *Lish and Jerry at the Shrine* Windsor Park and Stormont; *The Freedom of the City* Abbey Theatre & Lincoln Centre, New York; *As the Beast Sleeps* Peacock; *Hamlet* Abbey/Lyric co-production; *Hold Your Tongue, Hold Your Dead* Boston; *Juno and The Paycock, John Bull's Other Island, Conversations on a Homecoming, Animal Farm, Observe the Sons of Ulster Marching Towards the Somme* Lyric; *Binlids, Working Class Heroes, A Cold House* Dubbeljoint; *The Crock of Gold* Storytellers; *The Scarlet Web, Bog People, Cuchulain, To Hell with Faust* Big Telly; *Carthaginians* Greenwich, London; *Dealer's Choice* Prime Cut.

Vincent is an acclaimed radio and voice-over artist; his film and television credits include: *Mickeybo and Me, Life after Life, Lá Choronaithe, Soldier, De Valera, Rapunzel* and *O'Duffy.*

Writing credits include: *Inventors* Kabosh; *Citizen* Replay; *Puckoon* Big Telly – Irish tour and West End transfer; *Strike* ICTU; *North Nua, Pariahs* RTE Radio. He is an associate artist with the Global Arts Corps, a board member of Brassneck Theatre Company and a proud member of Equity.

Gerard McCabe | DIGGER BARNES

Gerard trained at Youth Action NI's Rainbow Factory School of Performing Arts.

Theatre credits include: *Jacque Brel is Alive and Well* Lyric Theatre; *A Midsummer Night's Dream* C21; *Fireworks* (young writers' scripts), *Swing State Cabaret* Tinderbox; *Pride and Prejudice, The Jungle Book* Lyric; *25th Annual Spelling Bee, Midsummers Night's Dream, Blue Remembered Hills* Bruiser; *Henry and Harriot* Kabosh; *The New Kid, Sinking* Replay; *The Comedy of Errors* Belfast Theatre Co; *iSpy* Big Telly; *Herons, Pvt. Wars* Pintsized Productions; *Jack and the Beanstalk, Peter Pan, Aladdin, Cinderella, Sleeping Beauty, Show White and the Seven Dwarfs* Millennium Forum; *Aladdin, Pinnochio* Waterfront Hall; *Cinderella, Sleeping Beauty* Market Place Theatre.

Gerard is also Artistic Director for Pintsized Productions, follow them @PintsizedNi

Miche Doherty | FORK THE CAT

Theatre credits include: *Catchpenny Twist, Northern Star, This Other City, The Sign of the Whale, Unhome* Tinderbox; *Bison* Theatreofpluck; *The Home Place, The Hypochondriac, The Weir, Macbeth, The Importance of Being Earnest* Lyric; *National Anthem* Ransom; *The Recruiting Officer, Heavenly Bodies, Tartuffe, The Tempest, The Doctor's Dilemma, Hubert Murray's Widow, The Comedy of Errors* Abbey; *The Silver Tassie* Almeida; *Our Country's Good* Theatr Clwyd; *Arcadia, Salomé, The Double Dealer* Gate, Dublin; *Dead Funny, The School for Scandal, Halloween Night, Northern Star, The Way of the World, Love and a Bottle, I Can't Get Started, Lady Windermere's Fan* Rough Magic.

TV credits include: *Valentine Falls, Father Ted* C4; *LOL, Dani's Castle* BBC.

Tara Lynne O'Neill | GERI SUE

Theatre credits include: *Fly Me to the Moon* Greenshoot; *Planet Belfast, Everything Between Us, Clean Room, No Place Like Home* Tinderbox; *Mistletoe and Crime, The Hypochondriac, Educating Rita, Of Mice and Men, Translations* and *Jane Eyre* Lyric Theatre; *Lay Up Yer Ends* Grand Opera House; *Somewhere Over the Balcony, Liverpool Boat* Red Lead; *Translations* Ouroboros; *The Session* Dubblejoint Irish Tour; *A Midsummers Night's Dream* Bruiser; *Cyrano de Bergerac* Gate Theatre; *Forging Ahead* Replay; and over 18 pantomimes both in Belfast and Dublin.

TV and film credits include: *FARR* RTE Storyland; *Insulin Line of Duty 2, At the Water's Edge, The Fall* BBC; *Made in Belfast, Six Degrees, The Dinner Party, Full Circle* (Winner Best Actress, Cherbourg Film Festival), *The Roman Spring of Mrs Stone, Bobby's Girl* HBO; *Last Christmas, KAOS, Disco Pigs, The Most Fertile Man in Ireland, Wild about Harry, At Death's Door* (Fuji Award), *Nothing Personal, Touched by an Angel* CBS; *Teenage Kicks* Buena Vista ITV.

Radio credits include: *The Quartet, Wee Black Bees by Little John Nee, Grenades* (Gold Medal in NY Festivals Radio Awards and top prize in the Drama category of the PPI Radio Awards), *Midsummers Night's Dream* RTE; *The Reign of Joseph Cain* BBC.

Tony Flynn | PRIEST

Theatre credits include: *Romeo and Juliet* Sherman Cymru, Cardiff; *The Seafarer* Lyric/Perth Theatre Co Production; *Twelfth Night* Perth Theatre; *Over the Bridge* Greenshoot Productions; *Arguments For Terrorism* Oran Mor Glasgow; *The Winners* Ransom; *The Duke of Hope* Tinderbox; *Animal Farm* Peter Hall Season, Theatre Royal Bath; *Much Ado About Nothing, Miss Julie* Lyric, Belfast; *The Threepenny Opera, Faustus* Bruiser; *Making History,*

Macbeth, Amadeus Ouroboros, Dublin; *Massacre At Paris, Early Morning* Bedrock; *The Queen and Peacock* Red Kettle; *Measure for Measure* Loose Canon; *Streetcar and Car Show* Corn Exchange; *The Blue Macushla* Druid; *Mademoiselle Flic Flac* Pan Pan; *Torch Song Trilogy* Muted Cupid; *Jaques Brel Is Alive and Well and Living In Paris* Andrews Lane Theatre; *Alice in Funderland, The Plough and the Stars* (national and UK tour), *Living Quarters, Sisters and Brothers, Toupees and Snare Drums, At Swim Two Birds, Melonfarmer, The Papar, Respond, Tarry Flynn, The Hostage* Abbey Theatre.

Film and TV credits include: *The Fall 2* BBC; *Small Island* BBC; *The Tudors* Showtime; *Legend* RTE; *Proof II* RTE; *Pulling Moves* BBC; *Bloody Sunday* January Films; *DDU* RTE; *Glenroe* RTE; *The General* Merlin Films; *The Ambassador* BBC; *Some Mothers Son* Septon Productions.

Abbie Spallen | PLAYWRIGHT

Abbie Spallen is a multi-award-winning writer, actor and film producer. Her awards as writer include the Stewart Parker major award, the Tony Doyle Award, the Susan Smith Blackburn Prize, the Clare McIntyre Bursary from The Royal Court, the Peggy Ramsay Award, the Dublin City Council Bursary for Literature and the HALMA Foundation Award for excellence in the European arts. Her plays include *Abeyance* (Druid Debut, Druid Theatre Co), *Pumpgirl* (Bush/Traverse/Manhattan Theatre Club), which won the 2007 Susan Smith Blackburn Award, the Stewart Parker Award and was nominated for the *Irish Times* Best New Play, *Strandline* (Fishamble) which was shortlisted for the Susan Smith Blackburn Award and nominated for the Meyer Whitworth Award, and *Bogwog* (NPC, O'Neill Centre Connecticut).

Her short plays include *Thirteen* (Women in Power and Politics, Tricycle Theatre), *Shaving the Pickle* (59E59 NYC) and *Rubberfoot* (Pentabus). Her work is published by Faber and Faber and has been translated into many languages and produced across Europe and the USA. She has completed one attachment to the Royal National Theatre and two to the Royal Court. In 2013 she was writer in residence in the Lyric Theatre Belfast. Her work for radio includes *Rapture Frequency* (The Wire R3), *Live from the Palace* (R4) and the forthcoming *Snake Oil* (R4).

Film and television includes *Pumpgirl* (PG Films/NI Screen); *Seacht* (Stirling Productions)' and *Collusion* (Sharp Focus for Calipo). She is currently under commission to the Royal National Theatre, the Lyric Belfast and the Tricycle Theatre London and in 2014 was awarded the Major Individual Artist Award by the Arts Council of Northern Ireland.

Michael Duke | DIRECTOR

Michael Duke has worked widely as a writer and director in Europe, America, and Scotland, where he was Associate Director of Dundee Rep. Since returning to Belfast, he directed the award winning production of *Observe the Sons of Ulster Marching Towards the Somme* at the Lyric Theatre, and in 2003 became Artistic Director of Tinderbox. Recent productions at Tinderbox include: the TRUE NORTH season of new writing, *The Sign of the Whale* and *Unhome* by Jimmy McAleavey, *Guidelines for a Long and Happy Life* by Paul Kennedy, *Planet Belfast* by Rosemary Jenkinson and *Summertime* by David Ireland.

As a writer he has worked regularly with Benchtours in Edinburgh, Melanie Stewart Dance Theater in Philadelphia, and Livingstone's Kabinet in Copenhagen. He wrote *Revenge* for Tinderbox in 2004, *The Gathering* for Theatre Abandon in 2009, and an adaptation of Brian Friel's *Translations* for BBC Radio 4 in 2010.

Hanna Slättne | DRAMATURG

Hanna Slättne is the Dramaturg and Literary Manager at Tinderbox Theatre Company, where she runs the dramaturgy strand of the company's activities: working with writers under commission, production dramaturgy, writers' development programmes such as The Writers Lab, playwriting workshops, script panel and Fireworks Tinderbox's annual Young Writers Programme. Hanna is a founder member of The Dramaturgs' Network.

Since arriving in Northern Ireland she has worked to provide wider support for writers at all levels in the region and collaborated with BBC Northern Ireland and Northern Ireland Screen to run events for writers across the different media.

Hanna has worked with many of the leading theatre companies as part of the Joint Sectoral Dramaturgy Project. She is dramaturg at the Space Programme, an interdisciplinary arts residency run by the Performance Corporation from 2008.

Ciaran Bagnall | SET & LIGHTING DESIGNER

Ciaran trained at the Welsh College of Music and Drama in Cardiff. Previous designs for Tinderbox include; *Unhome, Planet Belfast, Guidelines for a Long and Happy Life, True North; The Sign of the Whale, Sleep Eat Party, Alibi, The Gathering, The Virgin Father,* and *Bruised.*

Recent lighting designs include: *The Pillowman, Pentecost* Lyric Theatre, Belfast; *Perservance Drive* Bush Theatre, London; *Angel Meadow* HOME, Manchester, ANU Productions, Dublin; *A Taste of Honey* Hull Truck Theatre, national tour; *Quartet for 15 Chairs* MAC, Belfast; *Philadelphia, Here I Come!* Lyric Theatre, Belfast; *Wanted! Robin Hood* Lowry, Salford; *Much Ado about Nothing* RSC, Stratford upon Avon/Noël Coward Theatre, West End; *Arabian Nights* Lowry, Salford; *The Little Prince* Lyric Theatre, Belfast; *Robin Hood, Macbeth, Wizard of Oz, Sweeney Todd, Romeo and Juliet, East is East* Octagon Theatre, Bolton

Recent lighting and set designs include: *The God of Carnage* MAC, Belfast; *A View from the Bridge* Octagon, Bolton; *Cinderella* Hull Truck; *Neither Either* Liz Roche and Maiden Voyage Dance Company; *Villa, Discurso, Tejas Verdes* MAC, Belfast; *Twelfth Night* Octagon, Bolton; *Conquest of Happiness* European Tour; *Digging for Fire* Project Arts Center, Dublin; *Piaf, The Glass Menagerie, Tull, Of Mice and Men* Octagon Theatre, Bolton; *I Am my Own Wife* MAC, Belfast; *White Star of the North* Lyric Theatre, Belfast; *Shoot the Crow* Opera House, Belfast; *Snookered* Bush Theatre, London; *The Killing of Sister George* Arts Theatre, London; *Habeas Corpus, Secret Thoughts, Oleanna* Octagon Theatre, Bolton; *Slattery's Sago Saga* Dublin Theatre Festival 2011; *Swampoodle* Uline Arena, Washington DC; *Treemonisha* Pegasus Opera, UK national tour; *A Slight Ache* and *Landscape* Lyttelton Theatre, National Theatre, London

Ciaran is currently the set and lighting designer for the RSC's upcoming production of *Othello* in the Royal Shakespeare Theatre in Stratford upon Avon.

Deirdre Dwyer | COSTUME DESIGNER

Deirdre Dwyer trained in University College Cork (Drama and Theatre Studies and English) and at the Royal Welsh College of Music and Drama, Cardiff (Postgraduate Diploma in Theatre Design). She participated, as the Designer, in Rough Magic SEEDS3. She was awarded the first Pat Murray Bursary in 2009. She is a member of Broken Crow's Theatre Ensemble. Previous work includes designs for *Matched: An Everyman's Guide to Affairs of the Heart* Everyman Productions; *Between Trees and Water* Painted Bird Productions; *Jezebel* Rough Magic; *The Scarlet Letter* Conflicted; *Witches* Ruairí Donovan Choreography; *Bug* BrokenCrow, *Blátha Bána – White Blossoms* Graffiti Theatre Company; *Love All* Cheery Wild Productions; *Berlin Love Tour* Playgroup; *Melmoth the Wanderer* Big Telly; *Dancing at Lughnasa, Dealer's Choice* Linbury Studio Theatre, LAMDA, London; *West Side Story, Honk* Cork Opera House; *August: Ossage County* Bute Theatre, Cardiff. She has also designed for Waterford Spraoi, Clinic Media, MooCowProductions, Making Strange, Half/Angel and Little Red Kettle.

James Kennedy | SOUND DESIGNER

James is primarily a sound designer/composer, working also in production, technical and stage management. He studied music technology at Staffordshire University and has been working in theatre since.

Previous sound designs include: *Dirty Dancing at le Shabeen* Red Brick productions; *Slimmer for Christmas, Eternally Scrooged, Aladdin* Theatre at the Mill; *NI Opera Shorts 2012* NI Opera, *Titanic: Scenes from the British Wreck Commissioner's Inquiry, 1912* The MAC; *A Night in November* Grand Opera House; *Jack and the Beanstalk, Baby it's Cold Outside, Little Red Riding Hood, 50 Shades of Red White and Blue, The Titanic Boys, Fly Me to the Moon, Sleeping Beauty, Dancing Shoes, Christmas Eve Can Kill You, Stormont, The Interrogation of Ambrose Fogarty* and *A Night in November* GBL Productions; *Family Plot, Girls and Dolls, Duke of Hope, Sleep Eat Party, The Sign of the Whale, RJ's Leaving Day, Huzzies, Summertime* Tinderbox Theatre Company; *Protestants, The Half, The Early Bird, This Piece of Earth* and *Winners* Ransom Theatre Company; *The Liverpool Boat* and *The Iceberg* Red Lead Art; *5 in 1, The Lost Story Arc, To Have and to Hold* Kabosh; *Rock Doves* Rathmore Productions; *Diary of a Hunger Striker* Aisling Ghear; *As You Like It* Jigsaw Theatre Company; *Sleeping Beauty* Ulster Theatre Company; *50 Shades of Red White and Blue, Maggie, Paisley and Me, New York State of Mind* Green Shoot Productions; *Stitched Up, Choices, Little Red Riding Hood, Not a Game for Boys* C21 Productions. He has also composed the music for a knife crime performance for the Northern Ireland Office in conjunction with the PSNI, and several different productions with The KIC Project.

Conan McIvor | VIDEO DESIGNER

Conan McIvor is a filmmaker and video artist. His diverse practice spans from experimental film and video art to 'moving image' design for installation, theatre and performance. His work has been exhibited internationally in Trondheim, Sarajevo and Paris in a variety of exciting venues including a disused police station, freight container and sonic lab as well as traditional gallery spaces.

Damian Cox | PRODUCTION MANAGER

Damian Cox is from Fermanagh and has been working with Tinderbox for over 15 years on a freelance basis. Shows with Tinderbox include *No Place Like Home, Caught Red Handed, The Chairs, Revenge, Family Plot, Girls and Dolls, The Duke of Hope, The Sign of the Whale,* and *Guidelines for a Long and Happy Life.* Damian works in the Lyric Theatre as well as working as a freelance production manager and lighting designer. He has recently moved back to Belfast after working in the Millennium Forum in Derry/Londonderry as technical manager.

Noleen Stevenson | DEPUTY STAGE MANAGER

Noleen Stevenson graduated from Queens University Belfast in 2010 with a BA Hons in Drama.

Since graduating she has worked mainly as a freelance stage manager throughout Northern Ireland. Recent credits include Stage Manager *Titans*, *A Better Boy*, *Those You Pass on the Street* Kabosh; *Unhome* Tinderbox. She has also worked in various different roles within TV and film such as production secretary for the Jim Henson Company's first series of *Pajanimals* and more recently as the production designer for KGB's award winning film *Made in Belfast*.

Andrew Stanford | TECHNICAL STAGE MANAGER

Andrew Stanford, a graduate of Belfast Met, is an experienced stage manager, actor and sound designer, working both on and off stage for some of Northern Ireland's finest theatre companies. Notable productions include Tinderbox's *Guidelines for a Long and Happy life*, *Planet Belfast* and *Summertime* and Replay Theatre Company's *Closer* and *Bliss*.

Gerard McCorry | AUDIO ENGINEER

Gerard McCorry is a Music Technology graduate of the Sonic Arts Research Centre at Queen's University Belfast. He has had the pleasure of working on a wide variety of shows at the MAC and on tour, with highlights including *Quartet for Fifteen Chairs* Maiden Voyage; *Crows on the Wire* Verbal Arts Centre and *You'll Never Walk Alone: The Official History of Liverpool Football Club* Royal Court.

THANKS AND FUNDERS

Thanks to the Arts Council of Northern Ireland for assistance in the development of *Lally the Scut* through the Joint Sectoral Dramaturgy Project and to the actors involved in this process, including: Nika McGuigan, Ivan Little, Mary Moulds, Paul Mallon, Ian Beattie.

**Tinderbox Theatre Company and the MAC
would like to thank the following people and organisations
for their support and contribution in helping to make
this production of *Lally the Scut* possible:**

Gillian Mitchell, Damian Smyth, Kabosh Theatre Company, Lyric Theatre, Replay Theatre Company, Production Services Ireland, Wackiki, Alan Clarke, Steve Hobson, Aidan Conaghan, Eva and Daniel McKinless, Belfast Royal Academy, Orangefield Primary School, Holy Rosary Primary School, Edenbrooke Primary School, St Therese of Lisieux Primary School, Boyle's Home Bakery and Tesco Royal Avenue.

Lally the Scut is supported by the following organisations:

Lally the Scut

Abbie Spallen's plays include *Abeyance* (Druid), *Pumpgirl* (Bush/Traverse/Manhattan Theatre Club), which won the 2007 Susan Smith Blackburn Award, the Stewart Parker Award and was nominated for the *Irish Times* Best New Play; *Strandline* (Fishamble), which was shortlisted for the Susan Smith Blackburn Award and nominated for the Meyer Whitworth Award; *Bogwog* (NPC at O'Neill Centre Connecticut); and *Lally the Scut* (Tinderbox/Belfast). Her short plays include *Thirteen* (Women in Power and Politics, Tricycle Theatre), *Shaving the Pickle* (59E59, NYC) and *Rubberfoot* (Pentabus).

also by Abbie Spallen from Faber

PUMPGIRL
STRANDLINE

ABBIE SPALLEN

Lally the Scut

FABER & FABER

First published in 2015
by Faber and Faber Limited
74–77 Great Russell Street, London WC1B 3DA

Typeset by Country Setting, Kingsdown, Kent CT14 8ES
Printed in England by CPI Group (UK) Ltd, Croydon CR0 4YY

A CIP record for this book
is available from the British Library

ISBN 978-0-571-32644-0

2 4 6 8 10 9 7 5 3 1

Lally the Scut was first performed Downstairs at the MAC, Belfast, on 14 April 2015 with the following cast:

Lally Rosin Gallagher
Ellen Carol Moore
Francis Michael Condron
Rahab Maria Connolly
Owen Frank McCusker
Gavin Richard Clements
Bun McTasney Alan McKee
Daly the Male Vincent Higgins
Digger Barnes Gerard McCabe
Fork the Cat Miche Doherty
Geri Sue Tara Lynne O'Neill
Priest Tony Flynn

Directed by Michael Duke
Dramaturg Hanna Slättne
Set and lighting designed by Ciaran Bagnall
Costumes designed by Deirdre Dwyer
Sound Designer James Kennedy
Video Designer Conan McIvor
Voice and Accent Coach Peter Ballance

Characters

Lally
twenty-five

Francis
Lally's husband, mid-thirties

Ellen
Francis' mother, sixty

Owen
fifty

Gav
thirties

The Town

Bun McTasney

Daly the Male

Digger Barnes

Geri Sue

Fork the Cat

Rahab
Lally's mother

Priest

Compère

The play is set on the border between
Northern and Southern Ireland, on the Northern side,
round about now

In memory of my mother
Thelma Spallen

LALLY THE SCUT

Too much sacrifice can make
a stone of the heart.
W. B. Yeats

I've met the 'man in the street'.
And he's a cunt.
Sid Vicious

A forward slash (/) indicates a piece of dialogue being cut off by another.

A question without a question mark does not indicate a question but a statement disguised as a question, as in: 'Aren't you just great.' This means 'I neither care nor want to know that you're great, nor do I actually think so, in fact I most probably think the opposite.'

Act One

*Lights up. A field; not remotely like a bog. There is a
small hole in the ground, about a foot in diameter.
Ellen – sixty, caved, eyes like a 'cat scan' the rest like a
child – is on all fours at the hole, her bum in the air, her
head in the hole. There is a rifle at her side. Lally enters.
She is mid-twenties and about seven months pregnant;
she wears a white stretch mini-dress once glorious, now
muddy. She looks exhausted and throws down a shovel.
She stands, heaving with effort at one side of the stage,
looking out, expecting more than a baby.*

Ellen (*after a pause, pulling her head out of the hole*) What
did I come in here for?

Lally (*ignoring her and looking out*) I have to say there's
not much movement. Has everybody upped and died?

Ellen What do you expect, love? This place is a hole –

Lally Where the hell are the throngs?

Ellen – chock full of flatheaded gimps, do nothin' to help
anybody –

Lally Nobody's that big a streak of cruel. There must be
something wrong.

Ellen – do nothin' to help anybody. Help anybody out of
. . . nothin'.

Lally This is more than strange. God help *me*.

Pause. Lally looks out.

Ellen Is there any sign as yet? Or are ye not lookin' at all?

Lally Stop that.

II

Ellen Stop what? Who *are* you anyway?

Lally Pretendin'.

Ellen Who am *I*?

Lally You do not have . . . (*Turns to face her.*) You are not dotin' or demented or even a quarter ways deranged. You are only havin' people on. So . . . you can, while you're with me at least, not exhaust yourself tryin'.

Pause.

Ellen Is there any sign as yet? Or are ye not lookin' at all?

Lally SWEET JESUS AND HIS RUSTY NAILS! YES! I'm lookin'. Never over lookin', lookin' on a fuckin' *loop*. But what about yourself? Should you not be doin' something? Is it not your turn? To do, like, *something* yourself?

Ellen picks up a shovel.

Ellen (*muttering*) Well, I'd rather dig my own grave and take a header in –

Lally God help *me* stuck up here with a devious . . .

Ellen – than listen to any more of the 'Why me's?' outa' you. (*Beat, with mischief.*) Whoever the hell you are.

Lally turns as if to go after her. Ellen scarpers round the back of the small workman's tent. There is the noise of digging. Lally stays looking out for a few seconds. The digging is accompanied by groans of fatigue, very dramatic. Lally rolls her eyes.

Lally And more to the point, where the hell are *you*, ye useless hip-the-dip husband? Barnacle ye are! Blight on *me*!

She has a pair of toy binoculars. She lifts them and tries to look through. They're rubbish. She gives up and lifts the rifle to her eyes and tries to look out through the sights.

And how the hell does this thing work? All I can see is my own eyeball.

Ellen appears again, holding her back, all fatigued and dramatic.

Ellen I know a fellah got let off on a charge. He told the police his wife had shot herself in the leg by mistake. Shot herself twice, in the leg, by mistake.

Lally What, is that it? Did you make a sandcastle round there?

Ellen No sign? At all? No sign since I saw you last?

Lally Maybe I should just shoot myself. Twice. In the head. By mistake.

Ellen What use is it anyway, two women with no strength? Stuck up here and no men to give us a hand.

Lally Would now be a bad time to remind you that time wise we're at a bit of a push?

Ellen Away on you. Sure I might as well use a spoon. There's a shovel over there. There's a shovel round the back.

Lally (*pointing to her stomach*) Have you eyes in your head?

Ellen (*muttering*) Or would I be confusing you if I toul' you to go and take your pick?

There is a moment which seems no more than a domestic huff. Ellen, quite forcibly, takes the gun from Lally's hands. She moves to the edge of the stage and takes up Lally's previous position of lookout. Lally, on her way off to dig, stops at the hole and looks in, taking Ellen's previous position with her bum in the air.

Lally Quiet.

Ellen He's probably only fakin' it, doesn't want to listen to you . . .

Lally Too quiet. He'll want fed. What have we got to eat?

Ellen We've two Cornish pasties, a bag of broken biscuits and a flies'-graveyardy type of a bun. And yesterday's coconut fingers in a plastic bag someone's been at.

Lally Likes them, the fingers. (*A flicker of despair; real, cutting through the tone.*) Oh this is . . . this is . . .

Ellen Do you know, I stood in the bun shop for a full half-hour before the staff even let on I was there.

Lally (*recovering*) Aye well, maybe they knew ye.

Ellen No, this was pure evil. Stood there lookin' at me like I was a dirty scut.

Lally Ellen, where's the food?

Ellen (*ignoring her, not moving, lost in the martyrdom*) Bun McTasney the baker man comes out in his stripes and his fat sausage neck. Says he, 'Make it quick and get out. After what yous done, yous're not wanted here.'

Lally After we done what?

Ellen He was at my wedding. In fact if my memory serves me, it was him who made the cake.

Lally takes a coconut finger out of a plastic bag. She goes to a fishing rod sitting on the ground nearby and quickly places the coconut finger into a basket that's attached. It's a plastic, colourful basket. Child friendly.

Lally A heartless fellah like that needs burnin' down to the ground. Just give me half a chance.

Ellen It was a three-tier cake with an edible bride and groom on the top. They gave me a knife to cut it, silver foil on the handle.

Lally I'd toast his crumpets alright.

Ellen Knife in my hand, I looked down and seen blood. On the groove between the handle and the rest. You know that bit / the bit.

Lally (*not really listening*) Kinda man is he at all?

Ellen They must have been using it and they hadn'ta wiped it right. Dripped on my dress. And there was a lump. A bit of meat under the foil.

Lally Should have give you free food.

Ellen I felt it with the nub of my thumb. A gristly bit of meat hangin' off. I mind thinkin' as wedding omens go, that one was particularly impressive.

She turns and looks at Lally, who is about to lower down the basket.

Here, you keep feedin' him up, we'll never get the wee fucker out.

Lally snaps, glares at her, gets up and grabs the shovel. She looks like she could do some damage with it.

Who *are* ye.

Lally . . . bane of my . . . that's what ye are . . .

Ellen ignores her and looks out over the horizon again. Lally goes to leave and is stopped with . . .

Ellen (*something has caught her eye – something in the distance*) Did you ever see the like of that!

Lally What? Is it a chopper, is it that dog? Is it a long-lens camera, a photographer? There was a dog. Wandering about; mental-lookin' thing with an overbite / and all.

Ellen Away down the bypass. Calm down, nowhere near.

Lally (*frantic, looks towards the hole, real terror*) If you see a dog, shoot it. If you see a chopper, shoot it. If you didn't see a dog what did you see?

Ellen It's a magpie in a tree pickin' the eyes off an oul' bit of rat.

Lally A single magpie? In a tree? Is *that* some kind of an omen?

Ellen Well I'd have to say, and it's just my opinion that it's not lookin' great for the rat.

Lally glares at her, picks up the shovel and goes to storm/waddle off towards the dig. Ellen looks through the gun with a mischievous grin.

Oh look, Lally, there's a single magpie. How's this for 'sorrow', eh?

She shoots.

Lally Are you tryin' to make him fall? God help *me*.

Ellen looks at the gun as if it's just appeared in her hands. Drops it, rapid like. We begin to recognise the sound of a child crying. It is faint but can clearly be heard.

Lally Hangin' on by his fingers. Are you not listening to me?

Ellen Who are ye and what have I done now, has brung on the gnashing o' teeth?

Lally (*finally losing it*) Sweet mercy on his feet! God help me! For all my sins and here I am, stuck on the side of a hill in despair and ruination, waddling in my shift like Fat Frosty the fat fuckin' snowman with no one for help barring a registered useless husband and . . . and . . .

Ellen I'm here too.

Lally Oh yes. Stuck on the side of a hill with . . . *my mother-in-law*! And here. And here my own flesh and

blood, my son, wee tiny thing, innocent, jammed down
a hole like a cork in a bottle. And seemingly, no one for
miles giving a tinker's curse on account of wha? Some
style of a retribution for oul' fools whose bad luck is
ridiculous? Oh I might be just a bit of a way blighted.
It might be that there's a big fat dirty finger of years of
bad luck never over jabbin' and pokin' me right in the *eye*!

*The child's voice cries on. Slightly louder now. Lally
runs delicately, if a bit ridiculously, to the hole.*

We're here, love. Your granny Ellen and me are here.

Ellen And your daddy's comin' back soon. Can't think
what's keepin' him at all.

Lally (*into the hole, sarcastic*) Which should comfort you
no end I would think.

Ellen starts suddenly.

Ellen Someone's coming. (*Shouts out.*) Who *are* ye at all?

*Lally picks up the gun and points it out, looking
through the sights.*

Who is it? Is it them?

Lally (*exasperated*) Eyeball!

Ellen They've come up. I think they've come up. It'll all
be right now. This is where it starts! Now is when it
starts!

Lally What starts?

Ellen What starts?

Lally Shut up!

*A man appears. This is Francis, Lally's husband. He is
older than her, about thirty-five. He is slack-jawed
and low slung. The air around him is small. There is
a palpable feeling of disappointment from Lally and
Ellen.*

17

Francis Wha? What are you lookin' at me like that for? With the oul' accusatory face?

Lally Where's the rest? Builders and all.

Ellen The people who've come to help us . . . What, are they parkin' the car?

Francis Can you not see I'm in distress? Sure I'm all full of adrenaline and all. Lookit, my hands is shakin' –

Lally (*looking past him*) [*Where's the . . .*] diggers and digging men and heavy machinery and all . . .?

Francis takes out a newspaper and hands it to his mother. She opens it. It's a red-top newspaper with a large picture on the cover of her and Lally giving the fingers/pointing a gun to an aerial photographer. It also carries the headline TOWN PROBES SUSPICIOUS HOLE.

Francis The sweat's lashin' off me like stair rods. I've come from the house. There's a crowd outside our house.

Lally What are they doin' down there? It's up here they should be!

Francis Bun McTasney the baker man's taken on the role of orchestrator. Big apron on him, flour comin' off in puffs. They think we done this for show. Jesus, look, tremors . . .

Lally For show?

Ellen That explains the earlier reluctance to engage in a transaction.

Pause. They both look at her, slightly taken aback by the lack of being an eejit.

Francis This other fellah pushed forward and asked me why we done this on purpose!

Lally Who the hell would go around thinkin' that?

Francis It was just the one fellah askin' but the rest of them were all listening. Like he was elected. To go. Forward. They were quiet. Alfred Hitchcock quiet. Creepy. As. Fuck.

Ellen But they can't just stay down there. That's not what's supposed to happen. That's not what happened before.

Lally You didn't happen to bring a drill?

Francis They're not comin'! Not to help anyway!

Ellen Ah . . . (*Laughs.*) They're all round the corner! About to jump out, do a big boo.

They're not.

Lally Sweet Jesus!

Francis Oh, and there's a select gang in the pub cookin' up a mood for drivin' up and slappin' heads! The great and the good and the easily led . . . sayin' lightning doesn't strike twice. And Lally, they've a point . . .

Lally No they don't. It strikes twice. It's lightnin', it strikes where it fuckin' wants.

Francis I hid behind a pint hearing slabbers getting thick. Every drink's like petrol on them righteous flames. Drown themselves into a frenzy . . . come up here and run tracks through the lot of us.

Lally You went for a pint?

Francis The best offer I got? This fellah, this random oul' fellah says he knows another fellah out by Castleblaney. A fellah, born lackin' in a set of shoulderblades, has the look of a tapeworm about him . . .

Lally (*quietly*) A *pint*!

Francis There's an act he does in a nightclub; he can put his whole body through a tennis racquet. He can force his way down and grab a houl' of the child. But I think they're wrong and possibly not fully engaged with the situation. (*Starts to panic a bit.*) But a tennis racquet *is* bigger than a flood well. (*Measures the width in the air with his hands.*) And then he would get stuck and where'd we be? The two of them stuck down there and him blockin' off the air with his big dangly, flappy skin with no bones!

Ellen Well, that's it. That's it. That lightnin' bit has us damned.

Francis We'll just have to stay up here, make the best of the situation.

Lally There must be someone. One single body who's willin' to help. Maybe you couldn't see them through your *pint glass*.

Francis (*weakly, with a piece of paper in his hand*) They gave me that fellah's number. Maybe he has a smaller sibling.

Lally Or maybe, God help me, I'll have to find them myself.

Francis What? You can't go down there.

Ellen *You* can't go down there!

Lally They just need someone to appeal to their better natures. (*Snarky.*) Maybe I'll buy them a *round*.

Ellen You can't appeal to nobody. They won't like you.

Lally Why not?

Ellen You're not very . . . sympathetic.

Lally I can be . . . (*sympathetic*).

Ellen looks at her as if to say 'Aye, right?' There is a beat, then Lally hands her the gun.

Francis No! You'd be the big trophy. Hang the scut on the wall.

Lally Why don't you start diggin'? I'll take a skirt round; keep a lookout for shoulderless cunts.

Ellen, like clockwork, moves to the edge of the stage and takes up her previous lookout position. She looks very scared.

Francis You will stay up here; I'm your husband, that's an order.

Lally You put your feet up, darling. Have a bit of an oul' bun.

Francis I will! I'll stay up here, because I'm not as stupid as I look!

Lally I won't be put off my stride by Bun McTasney and his neck.

She goes to leave. Francis is in a huff.

Ellen Where's Frosty goin'?

Lally (*turning back to them, uncertain*) This girl's not afraid of no oul' bits of rats.

She leaves.

Transition. Lights up stage left. A woman of about forty appears. This is Rahab. Her face is shiny and cold like an altar rail. She kneels in prayer. She looks up to the heavens. At first her prayers are low, mumbling. They gradually become audible.

Rahab Amen, amen, and thank you and amen . . .

She blesses herself and gets up to go, thinks twice and stays. Her speech changes, becomes more chatty, conspiratorial.

Well, I was going to go but while I'm here . . . I have a good one for ye. (*She becomes all showbiz, a 'stand-up', serious turn.*) No seriously, you'll like it. (*Winks.*) What do you call . . . a Protestant minister . . . with a drug habit?

She goes to tell the punch line then stops as if interrupted.

No . . .

Same. Only a bit irritated.

No . . .

Same. Only very irritated.

Not that either, no. Look you're not supposed to actually . . . It's not a question. It's a joke? You do know what a gag is? Why do you do this? Every time. You're God. You're supposed to have a sense of humour. You're supposed to have invented the thing.

Pause.

No, you've spoiled it now. As *usual*, there's no point.

Pause.

(*Huffy.*) You call him . . . you call him a . . . a . . . Crystal Methodist.

Pause.

It *was*. Funny. Not now, thanks to you.

Pause.

Aye, well, you're no Dave Allen yerself.

Pause.

It's alright, I forgive you. I am benevolent. And bored. But . . . leading neatly in and its funny that we're on the subject of forgiveness. Now, these are your words, quite well writ, not that side-splitting but there you go but . . .

you know that 'trespasses' stuff; 'forgiving them who trespass against us?' Does that include gather-ups and yahoos and scuts? Like them? Like her, the Lally one? Because do you see her and the like of her? I find it very hard to . . .

Pause.

I know I should. I know! But I am merely a human. With flaws. I'm just clearing this up for future reference. I may be on the verge of a bit of an oul' sin. This is not a bad town. Greedy, corrupt, begrudging, perverted, malevolent and criminal, aye. But it's no Gomorrah; we still shoot gays. And one other thing we're not is thick. Most of us. I mean first of all she, the scut, goes and gets herself wedged down a well when she's a kid. And now twenty odd years later it happens again? AGAIN! To her son? I mean, they won't swallow that. That is an affront. Come to think of it, round here, quite a bit less than that is an affront.

Pause.

And mebbe it's not a coincidence! They're sayin' the child was tempted down with toys and slices of teddy-bear ham. (Beat.) You're gullible. Sheltered. You'd think you'da copped on by now that not everyone is a saint. Ach . . . (Finishing up.) Dear God in your infinite mercy bestow that mercy on that poor snatter-headed brat. An innocent snatter-headed brat we must do our best to pray for, oh yes, but not get our eyes wiped, oh no. Not. Eyes. Wiped. At. All. And not get took in by a shower of two-bit scuts. A-A-A-men and thank you and goodnight, you've been great. (Beat, showbiz.) No really. I'm here all week.

Transition. On the other half of the stage two men are making their way up a hill. Younger and older, they are Gavin and Owen, reporter and rookie. Owen, around

23

fifty, Northern Irish but with an English inflection in his
voice, has a paunch with which he punctuates every
important point. Gav, younger, English, is like a red
setter: annoying but basically tolerable through
prettiness. He has an ironic moustache.

Gav But in the back window of the car there is like,
another film. Projection. It's moving but it like, bears no
relation to what's going on inside the –

Owen Gavin. Is that your name? I don't like that name.

Gav – and Kirk Douglas, looking uncannily like his son.
Only . . . distorted. He's in the front with some rookie
reporter, new guy. Who is very, very *annoying*?

Owen I wonder if there can be. Anything possibly more
thrilling –

Gav But. But. He's turning the wheel of the car and –

Owen – than listening to a complete but secondhand
rundown –

Gav – the view from the back window stays the same!

Owen – of a film you've already seen.

> *Gav looks stung. Owen is trying to clean off his*
> *trousers.*

Look at this place. Have you ever seen such a mixture of
rock and this . . . mud? It's like brown glue. I feel like a
fly on a fly strip. What are they called? Fly . . .

Gav I didn't know you'd seen it. I didn't *assume* you'd
seen it. I'm not supposed to *assume*. Assumption is the
scourge of journalism.

Owen (*laughing quietly*) Who the hell told you that . . . ?

Gav And. It didn't do the business at the box office so
in fact to assume that you would have seen it would be
elitist and the promotion of elitism is *also* the . . .

Owen Fly . . . strip.

Gav As a matter of record, the facts would suggest that the American public weren't in the mood for a film quite as dark as *Ace in the Hole*. And it is very dark. I despaired. Especially when you consider the relative lightness of other Billy Wilder projects such as *Some Like It Hot* and . . .

Owen I've been dropped inside enemy lines in Iraq. Afraid, yes afraid, for my very life, but I can honestly say I've never come across mud quite as formidable as this.

Gav I've never watched a black-and-white film before.

Owen It's not a bog; you know where you are with a bog. This is pretty singular . . . peculiar as this . . .

Gav I'm going to download *way* more.

Owen (*looking at Gav*) What the hell am I doing here?

Gav And it's just so relevant but ohmagud . . . sooo depressing. And the journalists aren't realistic . . .

Owen The best of us. The ones with a heart. We ran screaming from this place . . . as soon as it was . . .

Gav I like to be entertained. And that thing about tragedy.

Owen (*still looking at him*) . . . Humanly and professionally . . . possible.

Gav If five hundred people die, it's not a story.

Owen Try thousands.

Gav But one person dies and it is. That is such an over-simplification.

Owen Thousands.

Gav (*beat, turning around*) Oh. That would be . . . oh that's a really awful story to tell. To sell. To tell. Are you alright? I was so upset.

Owen ignores him and tries to wipe the mud.

Owen Maybe it remembers its own.

Gav What? The . . . mud?

Owen Now a bog will throw up bodies every few hundred years, like reflux. Maybe this is a variation. This is the rising bile of the mewling Irish dead and ignored –

He keeps wiping. Gav looks around, a little bit freaked.

– clawing up my cargo pants, spreading over my thighs and poking in my ballsack for a handy pack of Gaviscon Express.

Gav Shut. Up.

Owen laughs. There is a pause.

(*Looking out.*) Well, I don't see what's wrong with the place. It's . . . nice.

Owen 'Oh yes, look Dymphna, there's an IKEA beside the airport.'

Gav I expected . . . Bosnia.

Owen I've spent weeks undercover in a firm of Chelsea football hooligans, afraid, yes afraid, for my very life but I can honestly say I've never come across a fucking shithole quite like I remember this.

Gav It is lovely and green.

Owen So is conjunctivitis.

Gav For some reason I pictured *here* in black and white.

Owen No, you're right. It could be anywhere now. Any shitty country full of shitty little towns.

Gav I distinctly remember in my research a black-and-white music video from some eighties band called Simple Minds.

Owen Full of shitty little shops with hilarious puns in the names.

Gav But I think that was just a reaction to *Through the Barricades* by Spandau Ballet?

Owen 'Facial Attraction', 'Lino Ritchie'.

Pause. Gav looks at him.

'Hannah and Her Scissors' . . .

Lally appears.

'No Woman, no Fry'.

Owen looks up.

Christ. Oh . . . oh . . .

He recognises her instantly. He is staggered. It's like someone turned on the lights.

Lally No Christ here.

Owen Hi . . . are you . . .? Are you frightened? Don't be . . .

Gav I'm frightened, me. You scared the shit out of me.

Lally I scared *you*? What kind of a fool does that make ye?

Owen Ha! Right? Isn't it muddy round here? I don't remember it being so . . . what do you call those things flies stick . . . you could get stuck . . . I'm –

Lally There's danger all around.

Gav Dude, what . . .

Owen Beautiful though. So *verdant*. I can't believe I'm here . . . and you. Oh you've got some on your dress. Mud. Here . . .

He goes to wipe her down.

27

Lally Get your stinkin' hands off my person. And mind you stand the pure fuck out of my way!

Gav . . . language is she speaking?

Owen Do you remember me?

Lally You're on my TV.

Gav Nope . . .

Owen I'm more than that.

Lally (*going to leave*) You talk too much.

Gav Not getting . . . a word.

Owen I remember you.

Gav (*beat, penny dropping*) Shit, is that *her*?

He starts to get his camera gear out.

Shock and awe, shock *and* awe!

Owen Calm down, Dymphna.

Lally Reporters isn't it?

Owen Yes.

Lally I left my gun behind.

Gav Gun?

Lally So, reporters, what can you do for me? And why've you decided to tramp up the hill?

Gav I got that, *gun*?

Lally Leave the safety of the town, new four-star hotel, carvery bar and grill. That's brave of ye, not like the rest, scared of two women on a hill.

Owen Oh they'll be up.

Gav They will, but we –

Owen – don't hang about, listening to rumours.

Lally Rumours?

Gav (*camera on*) Do you deny the rumours?

Owen You don't have to say a word.

Gav What?

Owen We're just here to help.

Gav Don't we get her to deny the rumours? Isn't that what we're here to do? The first rule of journalism is to get her to deny the rumours.

Owen What am I here to do?

Lally (*turning it on*) Because I do need help. Can you help me, mister? Help me save my poor, poor child from a death fit for a hunter's hound.

Gav Was that a denial? Oh for fuck's sake!

Owen The husband denied the rumours.

Lally (*snapping out of it*) He did what?

Gav When did he do that? Did I miss that?

Lally Yeah? Me too, Dymphna. When? Did I miss that one too?

Transition. Single spot on Francis. There is the sound of rain. He's outside. He's being interviewed on camera. Flashbulbs popping etc. He is defensive, hurried, under attack.

Francis Noh, noh, you see . . . you wouldn't want to pay no mind, missus, to what's said round here. (*All smiles, desperate.*) They're all a pack of cunts . . . Wha?

    Pause. His face drops.

What word? Oh. Sorry. It's just . . . that word is used round here as a term of . . . like hello . . . how you doin' you . . . (*Beat.*) Noh, don't go, I'll go again! I can . . . use an *alternative*, yeah? (*Beat, he is really defensive; jazz hands.*) Ready? Right. You wouldn't want to pay no mind to what people say round here. They're all . . . victims who are mentally disturbed by the trauma of thirty years of conflict . . . and jealous too. Jealous cu— victims. They're jealous on account of the two-part TV mini-series that was made the first time round; the time the wife fell down a well when she was a nipper. People think she got a ton of money for it. But it was only the BBC. Personally, I thought it almost gleefully overplotted and it might have missed a beat in the third act.

Pause. As if in answer to a question.

You see people round here . . . they love to think you're some kind of a *snob*. They stuck the *snob* label on a fellah I know, name of 'Drown the Dog' McCarten out by Ballyholland. And all he done was ask the Ra would they mind *not* storin' petrol bombs in the bus shelter outside his house. Here. Hang on. You might cut that out. I don't want to get 'Drown the Dog' into trouble. He's a good man . . . unless yer a dog. Where was I? Oh aye, it wasn't a classic mini-series but there was a song. Number four in the charts! (*Proud.*) We used to listen to it. We used to turn the radio over every Sunday from the short-wave police frequency and it made a fortune. But not for her. She didn't write it; Stock Aitken Waterman. Like, I play music. Gigs. I'm very good. I used to be in a band. We done cruise ships, *a* cruise ship and we did have a while in Finland. Aye. Well . . . I played the song up till recent. And I got a phone call one day from the Musicians' Union. About rights. Can you believe it? I had to pay rights to sing a song about my own wife. Stock Aitken Waterman. The double-barrleled cu— So that's why you'd be better not believing the people round here. Call ye a snob even though yer skint! There's no pot of gold in this game. No gold here. No rainbows either. Plenty of rain though. Enough for drownin' dogs.

Transition. Back to the hill.

Owen Well, after that, I would imagine you would probably be needing some help.

Lally I'll do anything you want, interview me. I'll cry in a photo.

Owen It's not as easy as you might think.

Lally Put me in the papers in a sympathetic fashion and then get me those men with a head for holes. What could be difficult about that?

Gav What could be more difficult?

Owen It's a question of perception.

Lally (*beat*) I'm guessing that neither of yous has a forklift on your persons.

Gav *Everyone*'s a judge.

Lally Then do me a favour and get the hell out of the road and let the distressed mother go on her way.

Owen Why do you think those other journalists are content, for now, with sniffing around in the town below?

Gav The shopping capital of Ireland.

Lally Because they don't want to get shot?

Owen Why the lack of sympathy for you? Distressed mother, like you say?

Lally I don't know and I don't care! I've no time to care! Because the worst thing is not the lack of air. You might think that but no. It is the dark. There's a thickness to it, (*Remembering.*) It's got skin and smells like it has seen things it *can't* ever forget. And its breath is on your face and you hold *your* breath and close your eyes tight because you know if it sees you looking, you'll grow that exact same look and for the rest of your life.

Owen God, you've grown up into a beautiful young woman.

Lally Have you ever closed your eyes in the dark? Why is that, mister, do you think?

Owen I didn't expect that. Not with . . .

Lally And the stinkin' taste and crunch of dirt stays with you –

Owen I remember your background, such a challenging beginning for any child.

Lally – stays for the rest of your life.

Owen But then the whole world fell in love with *you*. Felt the pain of it, the anguish, all for you . . .

Lally Really? I don't remember seeing them fuckin' jammed down there with me.

Owen It was a tremendous time.

Lally Are you trying to be funny? Comedian in the house?

Gav A child was in grave danger. A child nearly died.

Lally And that child, I think you'll find, would have actually been *me*.

Owen (*in for the kill*) And was there ever such a place cut with God's blunt breadknife as this? And would anyone have thought that a dogfight like that could have been paused for something so simple! For the first time, since the first arm was raised, the eyes of the world focused here and not for the usual shame. It was as if a higher power had lifted up a child –

Lally It was a fireman.

Owen (*shaking his head*) – had lifted you up and *placed* you down there. On *purpose*. For the first time there was a gimlet glimpse of the possibility of rehabilitation through a sustained . . . (*well-rehearsed*) cold compress of raw human emotion.

Lally That's good! Write that. You must have the like of that tattooed under yer eyelids!

Owen This place was tired. Tired of mayhem, tit for tat, murder and sheer bloody –

Gav 'And now I know what they're saying, as the drums begin to fade.'

Owen The height of the troubles, Lally.

Gav 'We made our love on wasteland . . .'

Lally Yes!

Owen (*without a trace of irony*) One of the *many* heights.

Gav 'And through the barricades.'

Pause. Lally looks at Gav like he's the dick he is. There is a palpable gear change.

Owen But now. Now! Times have changed now. Who would have believed? Thank *God*!

Gav Yes thank God, for some. But now, for others. Oh GOD!

Owen Beheadings and global panic. The world's gone up five gears. Terrorism has lost its manners. We're a long, long way from quaint little warning calls with the code name 'Brigadier'.

Gav A ceasefire for Christmas. How cute was that?

Owen But newsworthy.

Gav Yeah, unlike . . . now.

Owen Civilisation comes with a price. The North? Hasn't that been fixed?

Lally (*quietly*) Aye, you'd think . . .

Owen You have to be aware of your global and historical positioning. And that positioning . . . can fluctuate. People, viewers can become . . . fatigued.

Gav Shops with puns in the names.

Owen And then, when it's happened *twice*? People are naturally a bit suspicious.

Gav Once is tragedy . . . twice is farce.

Owen Not to mention shit for PR. Especially when there's the perception that you're . . . well . . .

Lally Trash.

Gav (*worse*) Regional.

Owen You see within days of a big story breaking, a received opinion emerges –

Gav Have you any idea, day to day, how many poor, poor, *poor* kids get globally, trapped down wells?

Owen – and it's to that received opinion that most journalists unthinkingly conform.

Gav And not just *wells*: pipes, guttering; any small confined space.

Owen Once that received view is established, it's very, very difficult to overthrow.

Gav Have you any proof that the child is actually down there?

Lally I beg your fuckin' pardon?

Owen There are so many precedents, Lally. Too much *fatigue* . . .

Gav We really are up to our necks in disparate children stuck down holes.

Lally I feel sick . . .

Gav In India with a kid called . . . something and those Chilean miners that popped out like a packet of Pez, there were millions in bets placed on them coming out alive or dead. People walked into a betting shop and placed a bet. A *bet*. How do you even *phrase* that? Is there an accumulator? Do you know? Can you tell me? Have you placed a bet?

Lally I'm gonna leave before I kill you.

She turns to leave.

Owen Wait.

Lally Fuckin' means test for a rescue.

Owen I said other journalists.

Lally Fuckin' Tony Hadley.

He grabs her. She turns.

Get off me or lose a leg!

Owen (*dropping her*) There's something, Lally, there's a thread. Feel it, between you and me.

She stays. Just about.

There is a famous photograph in a magazine called *National Geographic*. It's called 'The Girl with Green Eyes'. Have you heard of it?

Gav O.M.G.

Lally The magazine . . . or the picture?

Owen It was taken in Afghanistan by an American war photographer in the eighties. It was iconic. A symbol of hope, from a time of devastation. A lot like you.

Gav Genius.

Owen Some years later that same photographer went back to find her again. And he made a documentary about that. A documentary that sold to, among others CNN. But he did that, not, of course, because it sold to CNN, but because there was a link between them. A thread. She had been an Afghani girl. But he told her story . . . twice.

Lally Twice?

Owen Twice. You are this place. This is a chance for, God, I don't know? Can I get to see the new civilised land? Is there another glimpse of redemption here for all of us to see?

Lally I just want my kid. I'm not even sure that I know what you mean.

Gav He wants to complete the circle, Lally, oh, a chance to heal your land.

Owen looks her straight in the eyes.

Owen We are of this green, this mud.

He wipes mud on her face.

Gav Oh!

Owen (*expertly reeling on Gav, without dropping a beat*) Why don't you shut your face?

Gav Sorr— ?

Owen With your empathy masterclass from *Take a* fucking *Break*. You don't have a notion what it's like to be this woman or me or anyone else who's sprung up from this place . . . you . . . English cunt.

Lally looks at him. Then at Gav.

Middle-class English cunt.

Gav begins to look nervous.

He's a bit brave standing there. Isn't he? Judging us, the Irish . . . underclass.

Gav Dude, you live in Hampstead, you're way richer than –

Owen Unless we're having a big fat wedding they can all laugh at in the near future, his kind have no empathy for us.

Gav My kind?

Lally But this is a baby.

Owen I know! And I'm local! I'm as local as a lynching. (*Winks.*) I'm one of you . . . s. I saw Francis on the news and those red-top photographs and something inside me just . . .

Lally Oh you have, do you then, something inside?

Owen And *yes*, within days of a story breaking, a received view emerges and *yes*, that is the view to which *most ordinary* journalists conform –

Lally Are you the one that's decent? Oh I knew I'd find the one!

Owen – and yes, in this case it is a view that involves accusations of horrors.

Lally Horrors?

Owen But the good journalist, the diligent entity will find the real story! The story *of* the story. (*On a roll now.*) 'We name the guilty man'! 'Arrow points to defective part!'

Lally What horrors?

Owen I can take you forward *with* the new province, Lally. I can present you as civilised.

Lally (*beat*) I asked you what horrors? What are they saying about me?

Gav Oh, they're calling you the personification of evil and that you went and stuck your child down a well.

Owen Don't worry about that, my girl with . . . Are your eyes green?

Lally But I haven't done nothin'!

Gav So . . . then it's your husband that's the personification of evil and he stuck your child down a well.

Lally Francis? My Francis? Francis is as thick as a brick. Nobody pays any mind to him.

Owen But they are paying mind to him. And the awful thing is, I worry that I can only defend you. I think I can make you an icon. He's . . . well, he's him.

Lally So what do I do?

Owen (*beat*) Why . . . give me the why. That might do. Desperate people do desperate things, kind of . . . throwback to a horrific past. I'll do my best if you give me that. Yes, now that I . . . think of it I really have to have the . . . why.

Pause.

Lally My side of the story?

Owen (*laughs slightly*) You can call it that if you like . . .

Lally I think I know what you want.

Owen The story *of* the story.

Lally 'My life of hell' –

Gav Like a country and western ballad.

Lally I could, couldn't I, yeah?

Owen My good, good girl. Let's have a bit of oul' cyatharsis! In honour of our new way of thinking.

Pause.

Lally (*quietly*) Why don't you stick your camera up your hole and try and make a fillum of the big gapin' space where your spine should be.

She kicks him in the shin.

I'm away to that town. To find someone who really wants to help, not just a filchin' suck-the-blood like you!

Owen Jesus mother of God!

Lally The time I've wasted listening to you. Black down that hole sharpenin' teeth on my child's face.

Owen And you're going to tell them this was an accident? Twice? A cruel trick of fate?

Lally You should *see* my luck.

Owen My da once told me of a fellah from the bad old days who tried to get off on a charge. Told the police his wife had shot herself. Twice, in the head, by mistake.

She stops. Thinks, doubtful.

Lally He didn't get off?

Owen Not a chance.

Then she recovers and turns.

Lally Just so you know, I'm not scared of you nor no one comin' in your wake. You can send anyone you want to pry with dogs in chains even with an overbite, there's nothin' here to see. I'll go down that hill and find ones who'll help. One even will do and not even willing. I'll stick my two fingers in their eye sockets and haul them up on their knees. If they stop for a rest I'll give birth on their chest. We're not scared of no one, and I am especially not scared of you.

Owen Well, I'm sure you'll find someone sympathetic, in the new and gentle Ulster. (*To Gav.*) Why don't we head further on up the hill?

Lally I know two hoors when I see them, just lookin' for something evil to grab.

Owen stands looking at her. Gav heads up the hill.

Owen There is a language barrier after all.

Lally (*doubtful, out*) Even when you can see that there's nothing evil there.

Owen stares after as she leaves. Gav takes out a handkerchief and waves it as he begins to head in the other direction. He looks just like a priest at a massacre.

Transition. Lights up. Further down the hill a county meeting is being held in the open air. A man stands in the middle dressed in an apron. This is Bun McTasney, cheeks like poked dough. He is addressing a crowd. There are shouts and jeers. He has to make himself heard. A man stands with a golf club. He is angry. This is Daly the Male. Rahab is in her element, busy working the crowd.

Bun I just walked right up to the Francis fellah and asked him why they done it.

Daly No you didn't. That was me.

Bun I'm not afraid to be counted. I did what had to be done.

Daly Jesus Christ. Rewritin' history is that what you're at now?

Bun You should have seen his –

Daly Was me!

Rahab (*playing the crowd*) Would you look at the two fightin' men? What a pair of cocks.

Bun Oh yous are all indignation now, but as usual no indignation from yous then.

Daly I had the dogs and all ready to go up there and run slices through the lot of them.

Bun Yous were all standing with the look of an ostrich.

Daly There it is, I can feel it coming on.

Bun All standing with the look of an –

Daly No we weren't! That's it . . . it's . . . I feel it . . . yer roadkill now.

Rahab How many men from Ulster does it take to change a light bulb?

Daly Outrage. That's what I can feel. My right to Outrage! I find it starts as a tingle in my scrotal ridge and then travels its way right up my epididymides.

Bun (*beat*) There's *no* need for that.

Rahab Eleven!

Daly Don't take my outrage from me.

Bun I'm just trying to take a consensus. It's up to the good people here . . .

Rahab One man from Ulster to change the bulb, and ten to turn the house.

Cheers. She's a hit. Daly thinks it's him.

Daly You see? The consensus is we slap a few heads. Baseball bat wi' nails.

Bun As a representative and the first Catholic on the local borough council I feel it's my moral duty . . .

Rahab How many council workers does it take –

Daly String the hoorbags from a tree!

Rahab – to string a hoorbag from a tree?

Pause. Daly looks huffy.

None, cos the fellah with the rope has the day off today.

Daly Well I'm goin' up. I'll string the Francis one up myself. Just for bein' a waster. A singer. Outta. My. Taxes.

Rahab Huey Lewis and the News.

Bun (*laughs, slaps his thigh*) Huey Lewis and the Neeews. Now that is funny.

Rahab Well, you do have to laugh.

Laughs from the crowd.

Bun (*beaming*) Aye, you do.

Daly What use him and his singin'? How many hospital beds . . . ?!

Cheers.

Bun Well, as long as we all feel the same. Do we? Well, do we?

Rahab We've all had hard times.

Bun Oh yes, me? I was devastated to learn of the recent death of my poor first wife; my first wife way back in the nineties when I was the first Catholic on *any* board. I heard the poor woman died from starvation and poverty.

And then, there's the ongoing threat of bird flu and its continuous effect on my trade.

Daly You make buns.

Bun No one realises the knock-on effect. Pastry's made from eggs. People are potentially afraid of eggs. Potentially afraid of pastry. Terrified of a tray bake. I ask you.

Daly Hard times and no TV cameras or movie deals for us.

Bun The forms I had to fill to get my government subsidy.

Rahab Even though we're photogenic and very, very funny.

Cheers now from the crowd.

Daly (*whipping them up*) Is this not an outrage so it is?

Rahab And the child's probably under the bed!

Daly They're sayin' he was tempted down that hole with toys and slices of ham.

Rahab They done it for the publicity.

Bun Money.

Daly FAME!

Rahab What kind of a woman would go doin' the like of that?

Lally appears at the end of this. Rahab is the only one that notices her. They stare at each other during . . .

Bun (*as if it's a joke*) I don't know, what kind of a woman would go doin' the like of that?

Rahab Oh I'd say it'd be a stretch to call it human. Fuckin' animal in the house.

43

Bun Oh, you're serious. I thought that was a joke.

Rahab Serious? I've never been more.

Daly You see, give these people an inch and the next thing they're in yer house.

Bun And even *if* she's innocent –

Daly Runnin' up yer stairs, in yer bedroom, prayin' to Mecca and rapin' yer wife.

Bun – she should have kept an eye on her kid.

Rahab I mean, what kind of a mother can't keep an eye on her own kid?

Bun (*playing along, winking – again, as if this is a joke*) I don't know, what kind of a mother can't keep her eye on her own kid?

Rahab That wasn't a joke either.

Bun Ah, come on, but you . . . you're . . .

A beat, Daly turns round on Bun, slowly, gleefully, like a cat with its very first mouse.

Daly Actually, to think that's a joke, that's actually . . . *offensive.*

Bun (*genuinely terrified*) What? How am I offensive? She's the one who –

Daly Do you know what I am now? There it is? I am *offended.*

He advances, aggressive and thrilled to bits.

On behalf of mothers everywhere.

Bun You're not a mother.

Daly Being in *possession* of a mother of my own.

44

Bun OK! I apologise. In fact I'll phone your mother and /
apologise.

Daly You cunt.

*Daly suddenly notices Lally's there, which makes them
stop. There is a pause. Daly takes all this glee etc., and
drops it on Lally, without breaking a step.*

Daly Cunt. Now there *is* a cunt. You might want to
think of takin' yerself off.

Lally And miss the gentle sound of yous all patting me
on the back?

Daly starts to growl. Low. Nobody cares.

Bun What *can* you want?

*Daly turns to the audience, quietly, still growling.
Lally turns to the audience too.*

Lally (*trying*) Well . . . I don't think I've seen so many
good people, crammed into one town square.

Daly I would like to apologise for the uses of the word
'cunt'. They just slipped out.

Bun WHAT DO YOU WANT?

Daly And as I've just issued a heartfelt apology, don't
nobody *think* of writin' in.

Rahab You're not apologising to *her.*

Daly God no. I'd kill that cunt.

Rahab 'Mr Kipling' here's just asked you what is it do
you want?

Lally Well, I saw the cake shop was shut so I called up
here for an iced ring. What the hell do you think I want!

Rahab She thinks this is hilarious!

Daly And *guess* how that makes me feel!

Lally (*looking out at the audience, trying to sparkle*) There's the town, well how are you? Now *that is* a throng! Now, there's the council and the masons and responsible people with two homes and arsed to vote. There's you, there's yourself, sorry, I thought you were dead. Why there's Mr and Mrs Malachy Short with the suspiciously tall second son, now Malachy's returned after years on the run. And there's Mr McAllister, lives with his sister and likes to boil kittens for fun. Ah there's 'Rap the Door' Mitchell the sniper turned teacher, did you have a nice time in Kabul? And here's no-thumbs Craven the most unfortunate butcher whose pig farm in the eighties took innocent people straight down the mincer to hell. And aren't ye's all. Lookin' well?

Restlessness in the audience.

Rahab Oh for sure, that routine'll have them right in the palm of yer hand.

Lally And there's Paddy Grout, the tout turned road planner who'll be immortalised in his own bypass some day.

Rahab Talk about dyin' on your hole.

Lally And there's wee Minnie Hatchett who ran the safest house where half our government used to pee in a jar.

Rahab I hope you've a car runnin' outside, love, you'll not get out alive.

Lally Oh I don't mean to be rude, I know I'm addressing the great and the good and the glitter is comin' off ye's in stars. All I'm saying is that none of us here . . . has a pass on havin' done wrong.

The audience noise swells.

Like me, I'm no saint. I'd pick a fight with my foot. And there are women here I've punched. And men. And I'm proud. Not of that. I'm *too* proud. But I'll beg. (*On her knees.*) For help. For my son. Come with me, all you strong men. And all you women, some of which I've punched. And if yous knew my boy like me . . . spent even two bare seconds with him . . . because there isn't a more innocent or sweet wee thing who's never punched nothin'. My boy and his name / is . . .

Bun Look, there's nobody here saying your child isn't nice, or good lookin', or . . .

Daly Whatever the fuck . . .

Lally I knew all I needed was to let yous see him through me. I never knew such a love. I never knew it could be as strong. As strong as a ship. And now you see that, I know now you'll help me.

Pause.

So you will.

No reaction.

Strong as a ship.

Few shuffles. Coughs.

Bun We're in the middle of a meeting . . . about that very thing.

Lally Yes, all these people, here just for us! Just look at the glittery sparks.

Bun (*still awkward*) I suppose now that she's *arrived*, she can answer a few questions.

Lally But we need to go and get my baby. My baby whose name / is . . .

Bun I suppose in the interest of fairness.

Daly I've all the answers I need.

Lally But why are yous just sitting . . . (*Beat, twigging.*) All yous out there. Yous were gathered here. To . . . to . . . *not* to help!

Bun You don't seem to be aware of the terrible damage you've done to our positive steps in rebranding this town.

Lally This is . . . some sort of a *show*?

Bun If we rush to help the likes of you . . . the outside world's gonna implicate us.

Daly People are very judgemental. We're already misunderstood.

Rahab Especially our very dark sense of humour.

Bun But we are holding a meeting. And in the process of setting up a board.

Daly People who judge should be strung. Up.

Lally I think I might go mad.

Bun (*beat, adopting the voice of reason*) Now where exactly is this well? Is it the one in Cunningham's field?

Lally We don't know if anything's broken. He can't talk yet, just a bit slow.

Rahab In the Dulux colour chart of black, black humour we're down there with . . . Chernobyl.

Bun You see we're not exactly sure if that field, this being the border . . .

Lally And we can't tell if the screams are of pain or because he's scared on his own.

Bun We've Ordnance Survey maps and I've had to put in a few calls.

Lally In the dark.

Bun It's impossible to tell –

Rahab Pitch black.

Bun – if it's in the North or in the South.

Lally (*beat – she jerks her head up*) What?

Bun We were trying to establish if the field's in the North or in the South.

Lally What difference does that make?

Bun Well, if it's not in my jurisdiction, I can't just go digging around –

Daly You stupid pikey fuck.

Bun Cross-border initiatives is a nightmare to set up.

Lally I'm not a pikey.

Daly Stupid *picky* fuck then, Jesus.

Bun You have to contact the relevant parties . . . you can't stamp all over people's toes. Not on this bloody island.

Lally So should I be gettin' on a bus?

Bun You've no idea of the delicacy, the sensitivity I've had to portray.

Lally Head over the border? Right. (*Leaving.*) Wastin' my time!

Bun Well that's just lovely! And after I already took a major professional risk and sent a team of workers on up.

Lally (*stopping*) You did?

Rahab You did?

Daly You wha?

His phone suddenly beeps. He looks at it.

Bun Did you really think we were the type of town that would let a young boy die?

Daly Who give you th'authority to do the like of that?

Phones beep in the audience. Shuffles.

Bun As an elected representative of the local borough council and traders' and vintners' association, association of builders, retailers and ombudsmen of pretty much fucking everything, I weighed up the pros and cons and offset the cost of the operation and the chance that we might be held publicly responsible against the projected revenue and possibility that we might be held accountable, which is different, and I came up with a viable solution.

Lally Oh thank you. Thank you. Oh my God.

Bun I mean we're talking about a child here. Who do you think we are?

Daly You mean we don't get to go up there and pillage through the lot of them?

Lally Of course. You wouldn't just . . . (*Under her breath.*) Oh no, that would be *evil.*

Bun (*under his breath*) Not to mention the benefit a rescue will do for the projected revenue of the town.

Rahab What kind of people exactly do you think we are?

Daly . . . Rip their fucking heads off and take a collective shit down their necks?

Lally starts to laugh with relief.

Bun I done a feasibility study. And I decided that the appropriate thing to do would be to send up every help necessary. And all that despite the fact that I am grieving . . . my poor first wife.

Daly (*still miffed*) Well I wouldn't be surprised if there wasn't a few people already on their way up . . .

Shouts of 'Oh aye' from the audience. Sound of chairs moving.

Bun Oh, the tear-soaked pages. I had forms coming out my swiss roll.

Lally You're a very good man. Know you are a very good man.

Bun And it's not as if people are the most sympathetic to, well, you.

Lally And I'm sure, you bein' such a very good man, and important, you talked about the rescue. I'm sure you bein' the first Catholic on the board of everything you made sure that the crew will do the rescue right?

Pause. It's obvious from Bun's face that his feasibility study may have omitted this.

I'm sure ye's thrashed this out. The bit where they have to, in a rescue, dig down and then right underneath where he's wedged.

Bun Well, we . . .

Lally That they drill a tunnel parallel to the well he is stuck in but they have to keep drilling down until they're actually past where he is.

Bun Really.

Lally But of course that's not news to you. That they tunnel on down past where he is and that they then turn the drill and tunnel across. Down past where he is, and then across. Until you're underneath. Like an L shape. Yes? An L –

Daly I don't believe this.

Lally PLEASE DON'T GO UNDERESTIMATIN' THE IMPORTANCE OF WHAT I SAY!

Bun We have taken your points on board.

Lally And once they're underneath where he is, they have to put across a large iron bar. An iron bar across underneath WHERE HE IS WEDGED, but you know that. It is a *brace*.

Bun Your opinion is important to us and we'll get right back to you very soon.

Rahab Anything else you'd like, have him out at a certain time?

Lally The brace is to catch him. If he falls!

Daly Why don't you show a bit of gratitude? They'll go as fast as they can.

Lally I never mentioned fast. This is to *stop* him if he falls.

Bun Not to go as *fast* as they can would imply a certain level of cruelty.

Lally The worst thing you could do would be to tunnel just till you're alongside him. Then reach across and grab him, you'll break his fucking neck!

Daly And let it not be said by no slut and cunt that this is a cruel town.

Lally And the shock would definitely make him fall.

Bun After everything she's done, she thinks she can accuse us –

Lally But if there's a brace. I know a bit about this . . .

Rahab 'Do what I tell you, and get a move on', eh'

Lally A brace!

Bun – of not making the utmost haste in getting her brat out of that hole.

Lally I'm not!

Bun I mean why in the name of God, would anyone, anywhere want to take it slow?

Transition. Noise of digger. Lights up. Owen and Gav stand with a builder. This is Barnes, the pallor if not necessarily the size of a redbrick gable-end wall. There is a glow over his shoulder and shouts. It's obviously where all the work is taking place. Barnes is in a hard hat. He has a spare hard hat. He gives it to Owen. Gav gets ignored.

Owen Not an easy job.

Barnes Ah, it's not an easy job at all. Eh, hang on . . . am I bein' interviewed?

Owen Do you want to be –

Gav It's so great to see you here.

Barnes No! I'm just an ordinary fellah. I was just checkin', ye know?

Owen (*beat*) No, if you don't want to be. That's fine. We can just . . .

Gav Chitter chat.

Barnes (*looking a little relieved*) Aye, it's just . . . gettin' involved . . . (*He looks about him.*) You know? Ehm . . . well we've started OK with the equipment we were give. But if we hit a bit of granite . . . oh ho ho . . .

Owen That would be bad.

Gav It is absolutely brilliant to have a man just like you on board.

He goes to punch Barnes on the arm. Barnes looks at him like he's diseased.

Barnes Do I know you? I mean I know him, off me telly but . . .

Gav I feel like I know you.

Barnes Why, who's been talkin'?

Gav Nobody –

Owen You know you can trust me.

Gav – has a bad word to say about you. I promise.

Barnes stares at Gav, looking frightened. Owen gives Gav a 'shut up' look. Barnes decides to stick with it and therefore turns his whole body towards Owen. Gav feels a bit left out. Which brings on a 'bounce'.

Barnes You see, round here's a mixture of different types of rock. Over there, yer in the South which has yer basic, shaley sort. But on either side of here ye have mountains which is volcanic. Granite usually, but even with that, you can have layers, you know? Granite, shale, basalt, quartz, all layered in a whatever the fuck, aye.

Gav Like a . . . *mille-feuille.*

Barnes does his best not to look at Gav. So does Owen.

Barnes So far we've been lucky with the shale but if we hit the granite or even quartz –

Owen That would –

Gav – seriously slow down the dig?

Barnes It would . . .

Owen By how much?

Barnes You're talkin' hard-rock high-temperature drillin', you're talkin' an eight-bladed design; more diamond volume on the hole bottom, and enhanced management on the . . .

Reporters are reunited by both looking suitably blank.

Barnes You're talkin' expensive. And very slow. Why do yous' want to know?

Gav Well, the longer it takes, the more chance there is of finding the story . . .

Barnes What?

Owen covers up his need to strangle, just.

Well, that's a bit sick, don't you think? Longer. God . . . yous are sick alright –

Owen He doesn't mean *longer*.

Gav Have you ever seen a photograph called 'The Girl with Green –'

Barnes That's what he fuckin' said.

Owen Yes, it is. But that's not necessarily what he means. (*Looking at Gav.*) That would be callous and mercenary and the actions, frankly, of an *amoeba*.

Gav Oh dear God no, the thought of anything that may be of any detriment to little . . . to little . . .

Nobody helps him.

Pat . . . rick?

Barnes (*witheringly*) I don't think that's his name.

Owen (*to Gav*) No. (*Back to Barnes.*) But . . . it would be a silver lining, though, wouldn't it? If as a pure coincidence of what would, trust me, be an unwanted time . . . extension, that – that – *that* time period was

55

responsible for the *full* and *genuine* story about these poor people to come out?

Barnes Noh.

Owen OK. But what if, say, the rescue of . . . the poor wee cub . . . just happened to run alongside . . . human stories involving the players in this . . . ironic tragicomedy?

Barnes Would it not just be better all round if I was to put on a bit of a shimmy?

Gav We certainly weren't suggesting otherwise.

Barnes Yeah you fuckin' were.

Gav You really need to stop saying that.

Owen But don't get me wrong. I'm not talking about stories about the *family*. About *Lally*. Oh no, she's just more of . . . a cipher. What I'm really talking about are the stories about all the other ordinary people involved in the dig . . . such as yourself.

Pause.

Barnes Ah no, I'm just an ordinary fellah . . .

Gav You should never put yourself down.

Owen You're a hero. In fact. Now that I think of it, it was, in fact, the people round here who told us to come straight to you.

Barnes (*suddenly very very wary, scared even*) What? Really?

Owen Oh yes.

Barnes Round here? Have ye met them –

Gav They said such lovely things.

Barnes Round here!

Owen I never thought I'd see the day.

Pause. Gav starts to set up his camera. Barnes looks petrified.

Imagine how disappointed those good people will be, if you, the person they directed us to come to, turns round and rejects their recommendation.

Barnes Oh dear God! I might have fuckin' known!

Another pause. Camera now on. Barnes, still shitting himself, trying to hide his face.

Gav Five four three (*silent*) two one.

Barnes Well even if we don't hit granite, I need to point out that there is absolutely no guarantee –

Owen What did you say your building firm was called?

Barnes looks up, petrified. A sign appears, from above or from the wings: 'DIGGER BARNES, FOR ALL YOUR BUILDING NEEDS'.

Barnes But but but but, a thing like that, you'd be *advised* to . . . take a lot of care, wouldn't want to shake the wee man off his wee . . . you know? These things are not an exact science but you have to be . . . precise.

Owen In your expert opinion, tell us all about it.

Barnes Expert?! I'm . . . I'm . . . I'm . . . not . . . well . . . there's such a thing as soil displacement. Lack of . . . oxygen. And then there's . . . oh aye . . . Health and Safety.

Owen Health and Safety. So what you're saying is that it is a delicate operation?

Barnes Oh, I would say you're talking here in pretty exact terms about the difference between a procedure with a scalpel and one with a bit of an oul' laser. You fallah?

Owen And of course immaterial if you hit that granite, tell us about that.

Barnes Oh aye, the whole things immemmateral if you go and hit the . . .

There is a scraping sound behind them. The sound of a drill hitting rock. Sound of a drill bit splitting. Horrendous.

Granite.

He takes off his hat and stares up the hill.

Oh. I think I'd better be headin' up. I think that's a bit of a . . . you know.

He runs off.

Transition. Back at the county hall. They are packing up. Lifting chairs and moving round Lally as if she's nothing. Stage crew, dressed like townsfolk, men in stained T-shirts and tracky bottoms, women in orange tan make-up and pyjamas with high heels move lazily round the stage, clearing up. Rahab is still keeping the crowd happy.

Rahab Paddy Ulsterman and Paddy Romanian immigrant are walkin' through the forest.

Bun is on his mobile, laughing, obviously flirting, the one foot cocked like an eight-year-old girl. Lally gets a chair removed ungraciously from under her.

And up goes Paddy Romanian and tumbles down a hole.

Lally goes to Bun, who silences her with a gesture. Daly the Male suddenly stops what he is doing and looks out into the audience as if someone has got his attention.

And he says 'Paddy, Paddy, I can't get out, call me an ambulance quick.'

Daly jumps offstage and approaches a random audience member.

And Paddy Ulsterman looks down at him sittin' in the hole and says –

Daly looks to be in serious discussion with a random audience member. Lally gives up on Bun. She tries to talk to another stage crew member, gesticulating about the drilling procedure.

– 'You're an ambulance, you're an ambulance, now get the fuck out of our country, you gypsy cunt.'

Lally Oh what's the fucking point!

Rahab Do ye's get it? Do ye's?

Lally goes to leave and walks straight into Francis.

Lally What? What? What!

Rahab And you can use that joke again . . . substituting any Eastern European, minority or undesirable.

Lally What's happened! Why are you here!

Francis What? Oh. I was worried. What? I was. I was.

Lally I left you up there to mind him. I told you to stay where you were!

Francis Am I not allowed to be concerned about the welfare of my wife? I came down to see if you were OK . . . love. Are ye OK? (*He laughs nervously.*) Jesus. Stair rods. Look at that. I can hardly see!

Francis, sweating, takes a handkerchief out of his pocket to wipe his eyes. As he does, two betting slips, yellow, fall to the ground. All on stage stop dead. And look at him.

All on Stage (*except Bun, Lally and Francis*) Bettin' slips?

Francis What?

All on Stage (*except Bun, Lally and Francis*) BETTIN' SLIPS?

Bun Son. Did you get a tip?

Daly (*hearing this, thrilled*) What? Oh the outrage. The offence. (*To the audience member.*) Sorry, I have to go and kick someone's face.

He bounds back to the stage, advances on Francis.

Lally What are they? Gimme them. Did you come down here to make a bet?

Francis What? Noh. Them's is . . . Post-its. Wee yellah sticky . . . off the fridge.

Lally (*slow*) Tell me you didn't have a *brilliant* fucking idea.

He shakes his head, guilty as the man, and quickly picks up the slips and stuffs them back in his pocket. Everyone moves again. Daly backs off. Thwarted.

Francis I came down to see if you were OK. And there's builders and reporters and everything up there now. And don't worry, my ma's up there, safe and sound, makin' absolutely sure we're not misrepresented.

Ellen appears, then stops, as if she's forgotten what she came in for.

Keepin' a right beady eye on things. No better woman.

Lally Oh dear Jesus. Dear Jesus help *me*.

Ellen (*remembering*) Thon' builder up there says we've hit a big thick layer of granite.

Bun G . . . granite?

Ellen Says it's the thickest layer of granite he's ever seen in his puff.

Rahab Not as thick as you though, eh? Isn't that right, missus?

Ellen (*staring her down*) There's an expert up at the dig says what we need is an industrial drill, possibly with a carbide substrate for greater durability and thermal stability.

Bun (*to Ellen*) Could you . . . say that again?

He hangs up his phone. It immediately starts to ring (Kenny Rogers: 'The Gambler').

Lally Well, we can get one of them. Can't we get one of them?

Bun (*phone*) Hello, ah, yes. I just heard that, yes.

Ellen (*looking at Rahab*) Well, if it isn't lovely Rahab, the loudest laugh in the bar?

Bun (*phone*) Yes, well, that will be tricky. I'll have to . . . ascertain the procedure for that.

Daly the Male looks back out at the audience member. He nods and looks at his watch.

Lally Tricky? What's tricky about it? I mean, fuck the procedure. Hey!

Rahab (*to Ellen, taking the piss*) 'Who *are* ye?'

Ellen Oh I know *you* . . . and what ye done.

Rahab Shut your mouth!

She's about to leather into Ellen. Suddenly there is the sound of an explosion. They all turn and face out. Daly looks not very surprised.

Francis That's our house. You see? And yous were all thinkin' I was just on for the spoof!

There is the noise of cars revving up the bypass towards the dig. Lally is panicked by this. Everyone is.

*She goes to run off again. This time Francis constrains
her.*

Lally I told you to stay where you were. I told you that
for a reason!

Daly Oh well, great! That is *just* great.

*He starts to take off his clothes as he walks towards
the back of the stage.*

Francis (*watching Daly, suddenly smarter – sensing
danger, real*) Lally love, just stay where you are. Trust me
it's for your own good.

Ellen (*to Rahab*) The life and soul of the party. Always
the girl with the craic.

Daly (*grumbling*) My shift doesn't even start for half an
hour. I wasn't even ready.

Lally Get your . . . LET ME BE!

Francis Trust me, Lally. Now's not the time. Just put yer
head down and say nothin'.

*A stage crew member hands Daly a bag. Out of which
he takes trousers and a shirt.*

Daly Haven't warmed up, vocally.

Ellen The craic at someone else's expense . . . and look
what you did to your / child.

Rahab (*vicious*) Shut up!

Daly Enjoying myself I was there. Now I have to . . .
prematurely . . .

Bun There'll be a rational explanation for that explosion.
I personally guarantee it.

Daly Prematurely . . .

There's a switch. Daly now has on a 'Schools and Community Policing Liaison Officers' uniform and hat. It's suddenly as if he's a completely different person. Like something from a kid's cartoon. He also has a couple of glove puppets, one on each hand. They both look a bit like terrorists.

Daly I became a Schools and Community Liaison Officer to keep people safe.

Bun Ah for fuck's sake.

Daly And isn't it very good to know, that someone just like me can come and visit your children at their school?

Bun (*to Daly*) I take it there won't be a rational explanation for that explosion?

Daly And explain to them with the use of puppets the difficulties faced by the authorities in this vicinity.

Lally breaks free from Francis. She comes to the front of the stage.

Lally (*watching*) There's cars. There's ones in trucks. Swingin' lead. There's them.

Daly Now all of yous say hello to Colin the Continuity IRA dissident.

He waves the puppet on the right.

And this fellah is Real IRA Rory and a mad cunt with a hatchet.

He waves the puppet on the left – a little hatchet would be nice.

And Rory and Colin know a few other people, don't they? Like Oisin from Oglaigh Na Heireann and other assorted splinter groups, offshoots and factions particular to here.

Francis The house is well on fire now.

Daly So apart from just the usual gather-ups and yahoos you'd find in any town it's my job to *liaise* with those assorted splinter groups, offshoots and factions particular to here.

There is the sound of cars approaching – a dangerous sound. Aggressive, nameless.

Lally They're making their way up the bypass. Animals they are!

Daly (*listening to the puppets*) They're concerned!

Ellen How many salmon-faced hags does it take –

Daly But the thing about assorted splinter groups, offshoots and factions particular to here is that they're really very difficult to liaise *with*. And not only that but they do be dyin' for a scrap.

Ellen – to abandon their own child.

Daly (*coughs*) Unlike me. Being a figure of authority.

The puppets go mental.

They're a very bad bunch of doggies aren't they? And them bad doggies wants their piece of meat.

Bun (*to Daly*) You gave me a cast iron guarantee!

Daly You see Colin and Rory and Oisin are all just waiting for an excuse –

Rahab advances on Ellen.

– not being really prepared to live a quiet life just cos Mo Mowlam took her fuckin' wig off.

Rahab has Ellen by the hair. She brings her to the floor.

64

Rahab / You're dotin' love, as usual. Here, have yerself a rest.

Daly *Now* does everybody understand the exact meaning of the word 'disparate'.

Lally Can you smell them? I can.

Daly And 'splinter group'. And 'dissident'.

Francis That's an old familiar smell.

The revving is getting louder.

Lally Petrol and wet fur . . .

Daly Butchers, bakers and now mischief-makers. All come out to play.

Shouts, jeers, heading up the hill.

Francis And somethin' new I don't know . . .

The sound of car horns and boots on car roofs jumping and hollering. Terrifying. Triumphant.

Lally Do you hear that? God, what is that? A lock of known demons shakin' with glee. Taste of blood in the air. Taste it! God help *me*. All them feet. Nothin' delicate there. Big boots grindin' on small saplin' bone. Shakin' the earth. What will they do? Tell me! What are they going to do?

The noise is louder.

Daly It's only through the sustained effort of deeply rational people like me that all the Colins and Rorys are kept from itching. Through *liaising*. And then you lot go and scratch.

Lally Scratchin' at the ground.

She moves to the edge of the stage.

65

Daly This ground. Getting them excited. Don't you know it's a veritable tinderbox?

The puppets jump and dance with glee.

Look at them dancin'. Shall we all do the dance? Oh? What's that, Colin?

There is the noise of cars stopping further away, screeching to a halt; doors slamming. Footfalls, shouting, shrieking. All on stage are quite still. They stare out. From the side of the stage we hear chains running along the ground. Suddenly three very large black dogs run onstage. They get quite a way then stop with a jerk, the chains holding them back. They strain at the chains. They bark and rage at everything. Nobody on stage pays a blind bit of notice. Daly is listening to Colin. Lally moves to the edge of the stage.

Oh yes, that is correct. I must say I agree. (*Calmly, looking at Lally.*) Sometimes cunts like them, *was* put here to make my life extremely difficult.

He puts his hands down to his side and leaves in a huff. He may even point a puppet as he goes.

Lights snap to blackout.

Act Two

*Lights up. We are near the dig; there are a few lights
glowing over the hill. Digger Barnes sits exhausted,
eating a pie from Bun's shop. Francis appears with an old
tape recorder/CD player. He has been knocked about a
bit, has a few bruises etc. He puts down the player and
starts to strum on his guitar in a vain attempt to cheer
himself up. He presses 'play', strums the guitar and at the
end of every line of the following, a Stock Aitken
Waterman 'Ooh yeah' accompanies the song, which is a
pastiche of every Christy Moore song written, with the
addition of a disco beat. Francis gives it socks.*

Francis
   It was back in the dark days of Ulster
   In a place forty minutes from Belfast.
   United a country that prayed as they looked
   Down the well that a wee girl had fell . . . fast.
   It was cold and dank and dirty
   A space you could not chuck a twig in'.
   A poor wee mite half near dead with the fright.
   It was then that we started diggin'
   Diggin', diggin', diggin' diggin'.
   Aahdeldeedeldah.
     (*Ooh yeah*)

Chorus
   Like those who'd gone before us
   We picked up a shovel and then
   Started digging as only the Irish
   To bring back our Lally again.

   The cry came up, 'Come all ye men,'
   In a way that would make your skin clammy.

'Let's get this young lassie out of a hole
And back to the arms of her mammy.'
It was cold and dank and dirty,
A space you could not chuck a twig in'.
The poor wee shite half near dead with the fright.
It was then that we started diggin'
Diggin', diggin', diggin' diggin'.
Aahdeldeedeldah.
(*Ooh yeah*)

Chorus
Like those who'd gone before us
We picked up a shovel and then
Started digging as only the Irish
To bring back the wee girl again.

Repeat
Like those who'd gone before us
(*Ooh yeah*)
We picked up a shovel and then
(*Ooh yeah*)
Started digging as only the Irish
(*Ooh yeah*)
To bring back our Lally
To bring back our Lally
To bring back our Lally.
Diggin', diggin', diggin'
Diggin', diggin', diggin'
Diggin', diggin', diggin'
Diggin', diggin', diggin'
Diggin', diggin', diggin'
Diggin', dig-gin',
Aahdeldeedeldah.
(*Ooh yeah*)

*Francis ends with a painful strum. He looks over at
Barnes. Barnes keeps on eating. Francis puts down the
guitar and limps over towards him. He's starving.*

Francis Have you anything else there . . . you might want to share . . . in yer bag?

Barnes (*still at the munching.*) Fuck off.

Francis All free, were they, from the bun-makin' man?

Barnes Fuck off.

Francis I'm a martyr to an iced finger myself.

Barnes Are you hard of hearing? Are you normal deaf as well as tone deaf?

Francis There's no need to be like that. I used to play on a cruise.

Barnes I used to go to school with you; do you remember me at all?

Francis (*looking at him*) Eh . . . aye, of course, definitely I do. (*He doesn't.*)

Barnes What was this they called you . . .

Francis No they didn't.

Barnes (*starts to laugh*) 'Bungalow'. (*Beat, laugh.*) Fuckin' nothin' on top.

   Pause. Francis looks hurt.

(*Laughing, quietly.*) 'Bungalow'. (*Stops laughing. Looks at him.*) Noh, I don't sing on cruises, I'm just an ordinary fellah. But I remember you.

   Francis pulls up a something and sits down beside him. Barnes moves away a bit.

Francis How's it goin', like, how's it all –

Barnes Isn't it funny and ironic now, the way things is wont to change . . . me on TV. A vital part of a globally watched rescue operation. Your destiny in my hands.

Francis – up at the dig?

Barnes You don't remember the time, just off the top of your head . . . back in the day.

Francis Has he slipped . . . at all?

Barnes Fuckin' sandwiches weren't safe round you in them days neither.

Francis (*pause, remembering*) What? Noh. Me? Noh.

Barnes In fact, although not comin' down with cleverality, you used to manage to steal my lunch. (*Looks at him.*) Oh aye, you were the lunch-break terrorist –

Francis Must be somebody else.

Barnes – Gerry Adams with a Dairylea.

Francis Doesn't sound like –

Barnes 'With a sandwich box in one hand, and a can o' Lilt in the other.'

Francis Are ye sure.

Barnes My lunch that was made by the fair hand of my mother. Who died last year . . . of a *stroke*.

    Pause.

Funny. Wha? Me responsible for this whole rescue thing and me just an or-di-nary fellah. From yer *past*.

Francis A stroke? That's . . . that's . . . could you tell me . . . you couldn't tell me . . . sir, how it's goin' up at the dig?

Barnes Why don't you see for yourself? (*Smiling.*) Why don't you take a dander on up?

Francis I can't.

Barnes No. But you can steal food. Yer fuckin' *great* at that.

Francis Look, I'm sorry for stealin' yer sandwiches.

Barnes And you know why you can't go up, don't you? You . . .

Francis (*quiet*) We're barred.

Barnes It's not a pub.

Francis They won't . . . let us up.

Barnes That's right. And you know why that is, don't you? Bungalow fuckin' Bill.

Francis Because the town has . . . had the practicality to take it out of our hands.

Barnes And?

Francis And the community liaison officer had to step in and liaise –

Barnes – with them continuity stroke real IRA dissident boys who were proposing, among other things, the immediate attachment of your testicles to your forehead.

Francis (*instinctively rubbing either area*) Yeah . . .

Barnes But don't worry. Not as if this is a volatile area or anything. Yous just provoke who ye's like.

Francis Sorry.

Barnes Not as if we're on a knife edge or anything. Ah, we were all fuckin' bored wi' not gettin' blew up.

Pause.

You're very lucky. He hasn't slipped. He's fine.

He digs into his bag and takes out an iced finger. Francis looks at it. He looks at Francis and stuffs it into his mouth. He eats it and washes it down with a beer. Now would be the time for Francis to leave but he can't. After another pause.

Francis Some diggin' though, wha? Some oul' rock and all.

Barnes swigs his beer in reply.

That'd be . . . hard alright, even with the big new fancy drill the town got.

Barnes Hard.

Francis Tough.

Barnes Are you tryin' to be funny now! Is it the puns you're at, you one-storey fuck?

Francis Noh. Noh. Sure I wouldn't have the brain power. I was just wondering if you knew how long it would . . . (*Beat.*) I'm sorry about yer sandwiches. And yer ma. And . . . the very near recommencement of the conflict.

Barnes (*tuts*) We've to get through the granite, and even with the application of the newly acquired geo-pilot rotary steerable system – (*Laughs.*) Wasn't it great that they got that?

Francis Brilliant! Now . . .

Barnes And so ironic like, the speed with which one was ultimately found.

Francis Super, now . . . !

Barnes Once they got rid of yous. (*Beat.*) Anyway, now that we've managed to procure the right equipment we've still a fair lock of feet to go through.

Francis puts his hand in the pocket where the betting slips are.

Francis And that would . . . take . . . ?

Barnes just looks at him.

Two days . . . or three? Or even, or even . . . a bit longer? I mean . . . I bet . . .

Barnes You *bet*?

Francis (*drops the hand*) No . . . no . . . me? Bet nothin'
me.

Barnes Because I heard that there was a bit of oul' bettin'
going on.

Francis Jesus. Noh. That's . . . that's . . .

Barnes Because if it was tryin' to get inside information
outta me, in order to say, place a wager, as the ordinary
Joe in the street . . .

Francis Is yer name Joe.

Barnes I'd be under a definite obligation to reveal that to
my media contacts . . .

*Barnes is fishing in his bag for more food. He then
belches and decides he's not hungry and places the bag
at his side. Francis eyes it, then . . .*

Francis So . . . two, maybe three, you say.

Barnes (*watching him*) Something like that.

Francis, hand in pocket again, gets up to go.

But then there's all that bollocks about havin' to drill
underneath.

Hand drops again. Now freaked.

Francis *Bollocks?*

Barnes You probably don't know this but it *appears* that
in a shaft lodgement situation . . . where there is a
definite slippage factor –

Francis You have to put a big iron bar underneath.

Barnes – they have to get an iron bar and put that across
underneath . . .

Francis My wife fell down a hole.

Barnes That probably sounds a bit weird to you but we
know what we're doing.

Francis Were you listening to that song?

Barnes When you put that in, as a *brace*, there's a minimal chance of further slippage. Then there's less risk of whatyecallit, that there soil displacement.

Francis Aye, that's a cunt.

Barnes And much less of a chance of the nipper fallin' down.

Francis My son.

Builder So you get underneath him and I suppose you have to give him a poke but the theory is he'll just drop into your arms.

Francis A poke you say, drop you say.

Barnes Like a coconut.

Pause. Francis is speechless.

A coconut smellin' of shite.

Pause.

So don't you go worrying, we have the situation completely under control.

Pause.

Francis (*hating himself*) And . . . have you . . . any idea of how *long* . . . all of that would take?

Barnes We're on the home straight now. Should just take a few hours.

Pause.

Francis Could you be . . . a bit more precise?

Barnes (*smirking*) Well I wouldn't set my watch by it . . .

Pause.

Twelve midnight.

Francis Twelve . . .

Barnes I doubt there's a thing in the world could stop us from getting him out by then.

Francis (*barely audible*) Thanks.

Barnes picks up the bag as if to leave.

Barnes Not a thing in the world.

His phone rings. As he's getting it out.

(*Laughing.*) Here, what are the chances they'll call him 'coconut' from now on. (*Phone.*) Yeah? Wha?

He looks at Francis.

Who stopped it? Why?

Francis (*panicked*) What?

Barnes Why'd they do that? What cock did that?

Francis WHAT!

There is a pause. Barnes is now proper scared.

Barnes *Them* fellahs? What do *them* fellahs want? Jesus, we just got rid of the other . . . Aye, aye, I'd better.

Watching Francis the whole time, he walks off. Francis goes to follow him. Barnes turns as if to say that he can't. Barnes even hands him the bag of food. Francis stands there, impotent, the bag of food in one hand, the betting slips now out of his pocket and in his other hand. He looks at the slips, hating himself, drops the bag and takes out his phone and punches in a number.

Transition. Lights up. A huge tricolour dotted with sequins descends, dwarfing the stage. Geri Sue sits on a desk. Corporate, she is an ice blonde with Armani suits but can't quite shake an aura of dirty tights. Geri Sue's number two, Fork the Cat, stands at the back, frowning while reading Vaclav Havel's To the Castle and Back. It is imperative that he has a handlebar moustache. Lally rushes on. She has a rip in her dress and a smallish dirty bandage on her hand.

Lally Why've you stopped the dig? Why have you *fuckers* stopped the dig?

Geri Sue Who are you raising your voice in here?

Fork the Cat High girl, who the hell do you think you're callin' . . .

Geri Sue Do you think that it is appropriate till come flying in here like a . . .

Fork the Cat Are you trying to get yer head kicked in because that's what's gonna –

Lally I don't care actually because actually they just told me up there that yous *fuckers* have stopped the dig!

Fork the Cat (*triumphant*) And what proof do you actually have that this is anything to do with us?

Lally Because yous're the only local *fuckers* up there with flat white coffees and hand-stitched Italian leather shoes!

Pause. Geri Sue looks at Fork the Cat. Snared.

Geri Sue Well, as far as I am aware we didn't stop nothin' but if there was something that was . . . going that someone decided till have stopped, then I'm sure whatever it was, was stopped for a very good reason.

Pause.

Which is all you need to know . . .

She, in the course of dismissing Lally, makes a motion to Fork the Cat to pass her phone.

Goodbye.

Pause.

Fork the Cat She means fuck off.

Geri Sue That will have till do ye! We are very busy people. With a busy day. We have a Rebranding for Former People of Violence Now in the Process of Transitioning from Difficult Times of Transition into Equally Difficult Times of Adjustment workshop about till start in –

Lally I'm going fucking nowhere! Rebrand that, you cunt!

Fork the Cat (*genuinely shocked, each swear word hitting him like bullets*) Oh my . . . Oh my . . . oh. The language out of that! Oh that's just . . . heartbreakin'.

He then switches and steps towards Lally. He is real scary, not panto.

Lally (*sensing real danger*) I'm sorry. I'm . . . look, call him off. (*To Fork the Cat.*) Is yer book good.

Geri Sue Now look at me, dear. Look at me.

Lally What?

Geri Sue That's the girl, do as you're told. Because I am the only one standing right now between you and a severe mashing at the hands of our friend the throwback from the Village People here.

Fork the Cat What did you just call me!

Geri Sue Were you not about till put this woman in a stranglehold?

Fork the Cat Did you just call me a –

Geri Sue And are we not in a state of adjustment . . . of knowing that them things have all stopped?

Fork the Cat (*small*) Yes.

Geri Sue *Mar seo?* (*Well then?*)

He lets Lally go.

77

Maith thú a mhic. (*Good lad.*) See? You're let go. Even though you were buck stupid enough till come running in here like a . . . fuckin' dervish with haemorrhoids, lookit how we have dealt with the situation in a very, peaceful way. Because we are the face of a very peaceful . . . way. Take me for example, I am the new face of . . . all of it. Because we are a forward-thinking, newly *branded* party of equality and . . . are we not? Are we NOT?

Fork the Cat (*really trying*) Indeed we are.

Geri Sue Now I wonder if you realise how difficult this adjustment is till . . . do. And I also wonder if you know how difficult these times are till be doin' it *in*. Let me tell you at this particular time in the history of this precious . . . land, there's ones in this community who find themselves actually in *extremely* challenging times . . .

Lally Yes, we do. We do. And that's why I need you to restart / the –

Geri Sue I am referring, Jesus, till them brave people who have actually give *over* their former violent lives till a new dawn of peace and reconciliation.

Lally I don't know anything about that . . .

Geri Sue And isn't that just typical? Because you should know. Because it is the responsibility of . . . everyone, not just ones dedicated till the new dawn, to join us in adopting the acceptable face of rational . . . ality. Which means catchin' yerself on and not runnin' in here with a face on you like a screamin' fuckin' banshee.

Lally OK!

Geri Sue Give a body a heart . . . not to mention get your head blew . . . Jesus.

Fork the Cat Times of adjustment is very delicate, love.

Geri Sue Very delicate . . . and like any government

coping with that, we have certain challenges particular till . . . but then again similar till . . .

Lally Yes. And I feel your struggle. If we could get back to the matter / of

Geri Sue Take Czechoslovakia . . .

Lally What?

Geri Sue Take Czechoslovakia –

Lally Why would I want to do that?

Geri Sue – for example . . .

Lally What?

Fork the Cat (*slightly hysterical*) Fuckin' take it!

Lally (*nearly in tears*) Yes.

Geri Sue Or as it's now known the Czech Republic, havin' broke away from the Slovaks in 1993 . . . or . . . having got rid of the Communists in 1989 . . . take . . . that there fall of Ceausescu or . . . perestroika or –

Lally Oh dear God in his infinite misery.

Geri Sue – *any* former Communist place or ones that was under like, a dictatorship or totalitarian stranglehold . . . in fact any government like us who has till . . . come about under the shadow of what *was* a hostile stranglehold . . .

Lally Stranglehold, yes, yes, yes . . .

Geri Sue It is, however not nice, sometimes necessary till not only deal with a bunch of breakaway Continuity stroke Real IRA gather-ups and yahoos intent on unstabilisin' the stability, who you met earlier, but also, on top of that, to have to co-operate with them'nes from a former government. Even them'nes from what was like, a *hostile* government, in order till keep like, the smooth . . . adjustment into a . . . a

79

She snaps her fingers.

Fork the Cat Smooth?

Geri Sue I just said smooth. I can't use another –

Lally Stable.

Geri Sue (*beat*) Stable. Till . . . like, keep everything stable . . . in a new dawn.

Fork the Cat New*er* dawn?

Geri Sue (*patronisingly*) No. A *new* dawn for the people of . . . what are we using?

Fork the Cat Island.

Geri Sue . . . the *Island* of Ireland. In short . . . our old friend from the past . . . Fork the Cat here –

Lally looks at Fork the Cat.

– might know how to assemble an AK-47 or ex-Russian Army multiple rocket launcher with telescopic sights. But he doesn't, unfortunately, know fuck all about, say, all our water rates or . . . even that there proportional representation that has to do with . . . voting and all.

She stands waiting for applause.

But don't worry, you have me.

Lally My baby's about to choke to death down a well.

Geri Sue We know.

Lally You said you didn't.

Geri Sue No we didn't.

Lally So why have you stopped the dig?

Geri Sue Have we?

Lally Yes you have! Yes. Yes. YES, you fuckin' have!

Pause. Fork the Cat moves again. Geri Sue smiles and stops him, then gestures to him to bring over a map. Geri Sue places the map under a projector. She switches it on and looks at it. For a second she looks a bit puzzled. Fork the Cat watches her, then rolls his eyes and goes and places it the right way round. The map is projected on to the white part of the flag behind them. There are 'X's on it in red. Geri points at the 'X's.

Geri Sue What do you think they are?

Lally I . . . I . . . don't –

Fork the Cat At the risk of settin' the buildin' on fire, why don't you have a wee think.

There is an extremely long pause. Geri Sue plays with her phone. Fork the Cat nervously pretends to read his book, turning pages and scanning but checking in on Lally. Geri Sue shows Fork the Cat something funny on her phone. He laughs to humour her but then seethes with his book. A look of horror crosses Lally's face as she slowly, gradually realises what the 'X's stand for. Finally she's ready.

Geri Sue And now if you would like to take a look at the bottom right-hand corner.

Fork the Cat indicates two more 'X's.

You'll see that there are two 'X's, one of them in red *here*, and *here* one in blue. The one in red is a mark for . . . that there you have already worked out and the one in blue is for . . . where happens to be a certain piece of recent –

Fork the Cat – practically right on top, what are the chances of that?

Geri Sue (*tapping the projection*) Acquired. Drilling. Equipment.

Fork the Cat I was so careful. None of yer oul' bogs for me.

Geri Sue Breathe.

Fork the Cat I know, I know, but . . . why is this happening to me?

Geri Sue (*to Lally*) Now, love, as I am nearly blue in the face sayin', these are very difficult adjustable . . . times.

Lally looks up at the map.

Fork the Cat Tell her to stop lookin' at the map.

Lally She told me to –

Fork the Cat Fuckin' *memorisin'* the map.

Lally (*she faces him down*) I'm not!

Fork the Cat Look away from the map. LOOK AWAY FROM THAT FUCKING MAP!

She does. He whips it away.

Geri Sue As you can see, we could be on the verge of an embarrassing . . . incident for us all.

Lally I wouldn't be embarrassed.

Fork the Cat Don't you *dare* mock this procedure!

Geri Sue Oh but you should be, love. Because there are people around us at the moment who would jump to threaten the stableness of democratically elected local government.

Fork the Cat Don't *ever* fuck with democratically elected local government.

Geri Sue A vote for us is a vote for peace. And peace has to be protected. Democratically protected from all them cunts who would just love to put adjustin' and the new dawn and the whole . . . in peril and accuse us of bein' involved in –

Lally (*calling it*) What.

Fork the Cat (*really irritated now*) Fuckin' diggin'.

Geri Sue – anything that might *accidentally show up* while you'd be –

Fork the Cat – diggin' things up.

Geri Sue – the wrong unsettlin' of a bit of . . . soil in that area might bring up other unhappy, however like a coincidence, situations where our party's noble name might be linked to other unsettling . . .

Lally What.

Fork the Cat Diggin' up thems that was –

Geri Sue – unfortunate enough –

Lally What.

Fork the Cat – to get themselves fuckin' taken away by the likes of me in the middle of the night and buried in the . . . seventies. Are you thick?

Lally No. I'm not. (*Beat.*) I just wanted to hear you say it.

Pause. He advances, really about to kill her now. Geri Sue stops him with . . .

Geri Sue *ARAIS LEAT!* (*Get back!*) Didn't I tell you to let her be?

Fork the Cat But . . . she's . . . (*To Lally.*) I sat up in that field for three weeks, love, chippin' away, a master of disguise; a fuckin' hippy hat on me pretendin' to be an archaeologist!

Geri Sue Look, you need to watch yourself, love, as I only have so much control on those who really want to hang on to an older . . . deeply gay . . . way that has no place in the new . . .

Fork the Cat What do you mean, 'gay'?

Geri Sue Nothin'! We love the gays. Don't we? Relax the 'tache.

Fork the Cat (*really insecure now*) And what do you mean, 'no place'?

Geri Sue (*ignoring him*) But you are very lucky that *I* am here. Because I have an answer that might just be the answer to both our . . . challenges.

Lally What? What is it, for God's sake!

Geri Sue Never let it be said that we are the sort of people . . . who would put a child in danger.

Pause. Fork the Cat looks at her.

(*Hurriedly, like 'terms and conditions'.*) Unless of course that child is one of the regretted sacrifices made by many civilians and brave soldiers of freedom horribly caught up in the earlier difficult conflicts and often because of stuff out of our control and for which we are, as we always say, truly, truly, very, truly sorry.

Fork the Cat That *is* true.

Geri Sue In order to smoothly divert away from any possible bringin' up or referring to an embarrassing . . . to an embarrassing . . .

Lally Corpse of the disappeared.

Fork the Cat Dear . . . dear mother of God!

Pause.

Geri Sue What I would oppose –

Fork the Cat Propose.

Geri Sue Propose –

She snaps at Fork the Cat to show the map again. He does so, really irritated now and mindful to only show

84

*the bottom right-hand corner, quite petulantly shielding
the rest from Lally with his hands. And his book.*

– is to move the dig to the other side of the well. To the
other side of the well and indeed quite a bit away down
the hill from the well.

Fork the Cat points to an 'X' in green further down.

Right there where someone has already, weirdly, spooky
like, put that there 'X' in green.

Lally You mean start again? Missus, we don't have the
time.

Pause. Fork the Cat taps the projection.

I don't have any choice.

Geri Sue Oh there's always a choice . . . in the new
dawn. How far are you gone?

Lally What?

Geri Sue You could concentrate on the future of *that* one
and put any very regretted losses down to . . .

Fork the Cat We would like to just say we are truly, very,
truly sorry.

Lally (*terrified*) OK. OK. Yous can . . . move the dig.

Geri Sue (*sighs*) She thinks it's up to her.

Fork the Cat She thinks that's what she's here for.

Geri Sue We never need the likes of you.

Fork the Cat We would like you to pay a visit.

Geri Sue To someone who can help this . . . adjustment.

Fork the Cat What we need is for the blame not to be
on us.

Geri Sue The blame *isn't* on us.

Fork the Cat What blame? No blame here.

Geri Sue We need you to pay a visit to someone who can help us with . . . eh . . .

Fork the Cat *Rebranding* the reason for the move.

Geri Sue Oh . . . *bualadh bos!* ('*Clap hands*', *which she does*.) Well done!

Lally Why me?

Fork the Cat Why not you?

Geri Sue Isn't it about time you gave *us* some support?

Fork the Cat And after us just dealing with yer wee . . . problem.

Lally The wee problem wasn't mine.

Geri Sue What did I just say about goin' and apportioning blame?

Fork the Cat We just done you a favour.

Geri Sue And one thing we're all agreed on –

Fork the Cat – is that new fuckin' dawn or not, now or at any time we want –

Geri Sue – we can ask for favours of you.

Lally Favour . . . s.

Geri Sue A favour begets a favour.

Lally You just stuck an 's' on the end.

Geri Sue Did I?

Fork the Cat Never mind about that. Just run along and do this ewe thing and then we'll get yer chile out.

Pause.

Geri Sue And then you can concentrate on your health.

She puts her hand on Lally's stomach.

The young is, like, all we have –

She strokes her stomach.

– in the state of the future of the equal –

Lally – island.

Geri Sue Oh. Was that a wee kick? I think I felt a wee . . . Fork the Cat?

Fork the Cat comes over and puts his hand on Lally's stomach too.

Like I said, it's now up to *everybody* in the community to do their bit.

Lally is terrified.

Because who knows what . . . challenges the future's gonna throw up –

Fork the Cat In these –

Geri Sue – in these very difficult times of –

Lally – adjustment –

Geri Sue – that there.

Transition. A room criss-crossed in shafts of dusty white light. There is an echo and something to suggest a modern monastery; a very 'seventies' cross or a picture of a lamb, possibly with a sign in Irish saying 'Suffer little children to come unto me'. From stage right one of the black dogs from earlier runs on. For a second we think it is an accident; that it has gotten loose. It runs round the back of the stage and off.

After a few seconds, Lally enters and walks slap bang into Rahab who carries a tray of holy medals and a cash box and things.

Rahab We're not in!

Lally And this, of course, is exactly what I need right now.

Rahab I told you, we're not in! We're not in, now go away.

Lally Get the hell out of my way you bucket-mouthed oul' *polyp*.

Rahab (*suddenly really shifty*) Why are you here?

Lally Calm down, I've no dealings with you.

Rahab We're not in. There's nobody home. Don't you get it? There's no one here. Hasn't been for years. God's away, on his hol-i-days. No-body in!

Lally runs towards her as if to belt her. Stops.

Lally Are those pictures of my son?

Rahab swipes the tray to the side.

Rahab Only a photo.

Lally I'm glad the family album came to some use at last . . . Mother.

Rahab Keep your voice down, will you? You're nothin' to me.

Lally Why do I have to keep my voice down if there's nobody here?

Rahab I had a daughter once. Not the disappointment you turned out to be. Talentless you were. No charisma. With the comedy timing of a –

Lally And I need this too.

Rahab I had a daughter. I named her to be a star. I needed her to be a star. I named her Eulaliah. Not some Lally the scut. I named her after a saint, from a big write-up in Butler's who's who.

Lally The patron saint of torture victims, widows, and runaways.

88

Rahab She was some trouper. Better than you! She was brung by fightin' soldiers to kneel before the Holy Roman Emperor as that week's big star turn . . .

Lally Not a bit of wonder I ended up down a fuckin' hole.

Rahab Says he, 'Entertain me,' and says she, 'Noh, I'll keep my smarts for the Lord.' And the fightin' soldiers they tore her to the bone. Limb from limb with hooks of iron and burnt her with torches till she died . . . in a lovely repose –

Lally Wind it up there, Ma.

Rahab – and the heavens smiled; pleased with her turn and from out of her mouth a white dove appeared and upped and flew and then there was snow. And the Lord took her up to heaven and sat her down fornenst him. And there she sits and entertains him every day. (*Beat.*) With her craic.

Lally How lovely for him.

Rahab They think I'm a nice wee penitent. Don't tell them who you are.

Lally What are those? Are those relics?

Rahab I'm just a nice wee housekeeper now. I'm on to a wonderful thing.

Lally Are those relics? Tell me they're not.

Rahab It's only a bit of a nappy. To be honest it's not even his.

Lally You were never one to pass up an opportunity.

Rahab I said, you shut your mouth.

Lally I want to know why this is happening to *me*. I was just a baby. How could you put me down there?

Rahab (*beat*) There's nobody here! I've done my penance. Sure I'm great craic. Leave them alone! Don't you speak to them. They've enough to put up with . . . not about me anyway.

Lally (*going for her*) I've a great idea, Mammy, let's go play hide and seek.

Transition. Back up on the side of the hill near to the dig, Owen is going through some papers with Ellen. He looks a bit stunned.

Ellen They're just standard oul' contract things. (*Flirty.*) Off the information superhighway I believe.

Owen (*going through the contracts*) These are pretty extensive, Ellen: dramatic rights, song rights, computer game rights . . . computer game rights? Now that would be worth a patent. I'm thinking . . . (*Snorts.*) Baby Down a Minecraft?

Ellen (*dropping the flirt*) Aye, well, you just . . . (*sign them*).

Owen Were these Lally's idea?

Pause.

Do you know how extraordinary she is? I mean she's abrasive. But that doesn't mean . . .

Ellen She'd pick a fight with her foot.

Owen (*giggles*) She would. She would. But there's something else, isn't there? Something . . . is it resilience? Is that what it is?

Ellen Woman'll do anything to protect her own child.

Owen (*the contracts*) Ha! Won't they just?

Ellen Them's is just to protect us all, there's nothin'

untoward. There'll be ones makin' a fortune out of us, we've a right –

Owen Of course you do. And when I sign them should I give them back to Lally?

Ellen She doesn't need the bother . . .

Owen She doesn't know about them, does she?

Ellen Why don't you just gimme them back!

Owen No, I understand. I'm not. I'm not . . .

Ellen Aye, aye, ye are.

Owen You have to look out for yourself.

Ellen No. No. It was just us bein' . . .

Owen Us?

Ellen You're a cunt.

Owen You and Francis?

Ellen All of us. Lally, and the child. And . . . oh . . .

Owen Yes, *protecting* Lally. Well, thank you for coming to me.

Ellen (*to herself*) Yeah, that was a *great* idea. (*Slightly panicked.*) Sure I don't know what I'm doing. I've a head like a / sieve.

Owen I feel really honoured. You can tell Francis that.

Ellen It's because yer local. (*Beat.*) Francis?! No, it was all my . . . I trust you.

Owen (*trying really hard not to laugh*) Do ye?

Ellen Well I . . . fuckin' *did*.

Owen You know another thing I noticed about her? She's fucking good. Ellen, deep down, she's good. Is that what happens when you grow up in peacetime? I'm surprised she's let live. It's the difference, isn't it, between them ones who were born looking round corners and them ones who . . . weren't.

Pause.

Relax, Ellen, I'll sign your forms, and I'll keep them between you and me. (*He winks.*) And Francis.

Ellen You do what you like.

Owen Born lookin' round corners.

Ellen Well go on then, sign.

He folds them and puts them away.

Who are ye.

Owen Oh, an existential discourse! How marvellous. And you have no idea how much I've asked myself that since I arrived. Why didn't I hesitate? To return to a place I remember as insular, bovine and quite, quite joyously repressive.

Ellen Aye, we're all in raptures ye done that.

Owen I've spent nine months in Afghanistan filming through a slit in a burka. Afraid, yes afraid for my very life and I can honestly say I can't remember anywhere as insular, bovine and quite, quite joyously repressive as this.

Pause.

Ellen It's not so bad actually.

Owen (*laughing*) I looked back over the footage. I got friendly Gavin to trace it from the archives.

Ellen What footage?

Owen Of the first rescue. Lally's. Here, come on, have a look.

He takes out an iPad from his bag. Flicks to a film in front of her eyes.

Look at the wee baby, wee baby coming out of a hole.

Ellen Why am I watching this? Nothin' to do with me.

Owen Oh I know, I know. But . . . can you take yer eyes off it?

Sound of a rescue. Crowd. Isolated above the din are the screams of a baby in distress.

Listen to how much pain she's in. Unwatchable? Well, nearly, you know?

Ellen watches and listens.

The terror in her eyes being lifted from man to man. And now they're checking her over, to see if she's OK, managing *not* to spot that dislocated shoulder.

A sudden sharp child's scream.

And look there's her mother, look at that display of grief.

Ellen Aye.

Owen I thought I remembered a flash; the germ of a thought you know? Suspicion? Of something. But I was busy doing a reverse shot, which is basically a minute of me nodding. And that flash, whatever it was, left like it arrived. Because nodding is an art form. When you're that age and a twat.

The screams get even more distraught now. Ellen tries to look away. But she can't.

And now they give her to her mother. God, I think I fancied her.

The screams of distress are really loud now.

And there. There. Look, right there! Lally tries to get away from her own mother. Writhing like an eel despite the excruciating pain. She scrambles across a startled fireman so much so that she nearly falls. And the mother is embarrassed, angry. She grabs her, to quieten her. And she's covering, smiling at the camera, Ellen . . . as she grabs her by the dislocated arm.

A horrendous sound now. A child. Like an animal in pain.

And look at that child's face as we let her go. Straight back into the jaws of hell. And look, right up there in the corner, there's me. As if in affirmation to it all. Nodding like a cunt.

Pause.

(*Leaning in to her.*) If you think for one second I'm going to leave her like that again.

He snaps the iPad shut and away from her.

We could hold a contest. See who the child runs from? Now there's a story. Epic.

Ellen Rahab? (*Beat.*) Lally? (*Beat.*) Me?

Owen It's my considered opinion that he'll run away from Francis.

Pause.

Ellen You've no guarantee! What's yer guarantee? Oul' spoofer you are.

Owen That it will even happen? That we'll film a close-up of a child with its face as it squirms its way away from its monster of a father?

Ellen (*twigging*) Oh God. It doesn't matter, does it?

Owen I'm going to fucking write it anyway. He did it! I know he did! Lightnin' doesn't strike twice and he's the only one stupid enough. I've got my girl.

Ellen You've a notion of her!

Owen Don't be . . . ha . . . that's –

Ellen You'd make all of that up. Y'oul fool!

Owen I'm not going to nod like a cunt again.

Ellen About us.

Owen Yes I would.

Ellen The people from where you're from?

Owen *Indeed* I would.

Ellen You'd do that to her.

Owen *For* her.

Ellen Take all that away?

Owen Goodbye.

He goes to leave.

Ellen No matter what?

Owen What?

Ellen No matter what? Even if that wee child dies? Falls?

Owen Why would you ask that?

There is a moment. A flicker. The germ of an idea, a suspicion enters his head.

Ellen You'd be that cruel to her. Evil. The big flash reporter . . . even if that wee child, oh my God!

Owen Cruel? I'm not . . . (*And it's gone.*) I'm doing a good thing . . . and I'd do it *especially* if . . . in the event of that.

Ellen No, you're right. That's not cruel at all.

There is the screech of a megaphone.

Roadie (*megaphone – sounding bored*) Testing, one – two – three. One – two – three – 'sibilance'.

Owen (*quickly*) Of course I wouldn't write it if he . . . but he's not going to fall.

Ellen Well . . . at least there's that.

Owen They know what they're doing. This isn't about me.

Ellen No.

Roadie (*megaphone*) One – two. One – two. Ah . . . one – two . . .

Owen (*beat*) I'm trying to protect her. Here's news, Ellen, she just deserves better and nobody fucking cares. (*Leaving.*) I mean does anyone even know where the fuck she is now? What fresh hell is she stepping into?

Transition. Lally is still up at the monastery with her mother.

Lally Like old times' sake. You count. I'll hide somewhere bad. One two three . . .

Rahab That's it! I don't know you. I'll break every bone in your . . .

She grabs her, vicious. A Priest enters. He is a mess. He searches for something. Rahab backs down immediately.

Priest There really is no other possible explanation. POSSIBLE . . . POSSIBLE . . . If suffering is the under, or is it inner side of love, then . . . the presence of God in what might seem to the uninitiated, as a place where he only appears to be to *some* eyes vanquished and not present. (*Laughs slightly but hysterically.*) On holiday! But that's only the uninitiated. It is . . . to those who *believe* . . .

He stops dead, and picks up a set of barbed chains he spots lying to one side. He holds them delicately like he's been shot. He squeezes them. Then he forgets them as he spots Lally. He stares at her with a face full of terror.

Rahab It's OK. It's OK. She's . . . just –

Priest – dirty.

Rahab It's just mud.

Priest Why is it mud? And where did these come from?

He squeezes the chains. Blood drips on the floor.

Turn round.

Lally It's just mud. Look, I need to talk to you.

Priest TURN ROUND!

She does. He drops the chains and goes to her. His hand hovers at the base of her spine.

Is that, can you see, a slight distension in that –

Lally What?

Priest – sacrum.

Rahab No.

He moves back.

Priest What does she want? Did you tell her? There's nobody home.

Rahab I was just in fact this minute telling her that there's nobody home.

Priest Well then. Get her . . . (*Whispering loudly.*) Get her out of here.

Lally *You're* at home.

97

Priest She's talking to me.

Lally What the hell's wrong with him?

Priest Seems intent on talking to me!

Rahab You'd better watch your mouth, love, this is what's left of a man of God.

Lally Is there something wrong with him?

Priest You're not . . . you're not talking to *me*.

Rahab Look, if you like and it would give me a lot of pleasure, I can give her a slap.

Priest We don't slap people here!

He looks about shiftily.

(*Hisses.*) We do not slap people here.

Lally (*to herself*) There's plenty wrong with him. Now I know why they sent me.

Priest What did she just say?

Rahab Don't speak to me like that. I was only trying to help. If you're going to speak to me like that . . .

Lally Whatever crap this is. I don't have time for this crap.

Rahab goes to leave.

Rahab Just you remember, son, I'm the only friend you have.

Priest No! Stay here!

Rahab Yous are in no position at all to speak to *anyone* like that.

Priest Get her to turn around.

Rahab Not as if your image is actually that sparky as it stands.

Lally (*to Rahab*) If you stay I'll have to ask him to give you absolution for the past sin of wedging youngsters down confined spaces.

Priest (*to Lally*) Turn around again. TURN AROUND!

Rahab (*to Lally*) You keep your mouth shut.

Lally (*to Rahab*) Only if you get out.

She has to leave. The Priest looks distraught. He turns to Lally. As if she's a horror. He summons up courage. Tries to talk to her rationally.

Priest Last night I saw a black dog. I . . . did you ever see that sort of thing?

Lally Plenty. There's something I need you to do.

Priest Oh yes. You're right. How *does* that sound? But I believe it was – (*whispers*) *in the corner of my room*! I wondered how it got there as I'm so high up. We like to be elevated . . . then I saw its feet of iron . . . barbed. And that's how . . . with sloughing chains it scaled the side of this building . . . it looked at me and I saw the barbs and the barbs shifted and it was gone.

Lally You've been in here a while.

Priest Was that you?

Lally Do you want it to be me?

Priest We're all in a state of heightened anticipation. The poor child in danger, did you hear?

Lally That's why I'm here, could you listen for a second?

Priest At any other time, we'd be up there too. We love a bit of carnage. We were always available, in the dark days to give succour and good face.

Lally The dark days. Them again.

Priest Now there's nothing to distract from us. And we need a distraction. But now nobody needs our help, our prayers . . . over blood. The bigger picture has got very small, magnifying what . . . we did.

He looks at her, shamed.

These are such difficult times for us. Evil is among us. Focusing in on *us*. And we keep getting told that with the shedding of blood comes the remission of sin. But how can we, when in times of peace there is no blood over which to be observed; benign, giving profile.

Lally What sort of profile?

Priest And this would be perfect! A gift. It is a gift.

Lally This isn't a gift. This isn't –

Priest Even if at its root is an act so seemingly vile.

Lally – a gift.

Priest From God. For the forgiveness of sin. What kind of a mother could do that to her own child?

Pause. He twigs. Then looks at her. Hard.

So that's who you are.

Lally (*snapping back control*) There's a well.

Priest Were you told to do it? What form did it take?

Lally There's a dig. At the well. I can take you up there. (*Beat.*) It *is* a gift.

Priest What?

Lally It is a gift. I'm here to tell you that. And I can get you seen. Seen to be giving aid. We can get you in a photo. Absolving me. I will tell them that I have to have my priest.

Pause.

Have you ever seen a girl with green eyes?

Priest What?

Lally Fuck that. Nothing. I can do it for you. I know what has to be done, what you need, but then what I need is for you to get them to move the dig.

Priest Without the shedding of blood there is no remission of our sin . . .

Lally Yeah, I got that, fuck. Now, you will say that it is because it's a holy well. And there's less *damage* if you dig from the other side.

Priest There's no holy well there. There's nothing holy up there yet! Who –

Lally Men who sent me here. Well, there's a woman but she is an almighty dick so, 'Fighting Roman Men', who've done business with you in the past?

He stops, suddenly very wary.

Aye. They're really pretty sensitive as it goes. They would prefer you *till* make a gesture *till* old times' sake. But don't worry. Don't shit yourself. I can make you look really good.

Pause. The Priest is staring at the floor.

Hey, priest. Are you listening to me?

Priest Can you hear that?

Lally Can I go back and tell them that you've agreed to what they –

Priest Stop pissing about and listen.

Lally I need to give them an answer. They were pretty definite, you know?

Priest No! Shut up! Listen! It's as loud as fuck!

Lally I don't care! No! I can't hear anything.

Priest (*slightly hysterical*) I'm the only one here.

Lally Then let me take you away –

He goes to her. Weeping.

Priest I'm the only one here.

Lally – make one of them icons out of you.

He lifts his head and looks at her. Suddenly there is the ferocious sound of the chained feet of a large animal, running on marble. The priest turns his head, quite feral himself.

Priest That!

The sound gets louder.

Lally I don't hear nothin'.

Priest Hear that, you stupid bitch! Surely you can hear that!

There is a pause. He grabs his head in his two hands as if he might wrench it off. The noise gets louder. We hear something, at the door. Something not human. The Priest runs to the door. His face is a picture of absolute terror. Lally hears nothing. The Priest turns to her. Looks at her as if she is evil. Something thumps at the door. A noise as if a large beast is hurling itself at the door again and again. The Priest sinks to the floor in paroxysms of fright. Suddenly the noise abates. There is a hiss as the sound evaporates backwards and away.

Priest I should dig a hole too.

Lally You don't have to.

Priest So much innuendo. And on and on. Missives, memos about the damage. As if it's *all* down to me! Yes. Better to take it all and –

Lally You're just the same as me.

Priest The children. The children.

Lally Let me help you. A reporter told me how.

Priest Push it all underground. Until the blood starts to flow here again.

Lally Fuckit! There's no more time!

Priest Dear Christ, like a vault. They'll love that!

Lally HELP ME!

Priest Oh they'd go for that. A Vatican vault. The scandal, keep it buried.

Lally I'll get you in a picture.

Priest I'd like that. They would too.

Lally Of course they would.

Priest Sometimes I practise my best side.

Lally Great, now come on.

Priest I'm so lonely.

Lally Come on to fuck.

Priest It was supposed to flow again. It is Ulster. It always does.

Lally Let's go.

Priest What age are you?

Lally Let me help you.

Priest Help me. What age?

Pause.

Lally My . . . ?

Priest Are you . . .

Lally If I tell you, can we go?

Priest No, don't tell me. You look young. Young enough.

Lally (*softly, twigging*) Yeah. Lucky me.

Priest It's very kind of you.

There is a pause.

Are you shaved?

Pause.

You're that type of young woman, aren't you? So, it follows that you'd like it shaved.

She looks at him then lifts her dress as far as the bottom of her bump. She is naked. Shaved. He stares.

Oh.

He moves a step towards her.
He moves a second step towards her.

It's just not right, is it . . . that I'm the only one here . . .

He moves behind her.

IS IT!

Lally No.

Priest (*aroused, small*) . . . Oh. (*Beat.*) Because it is a spiritual wasteland that has grown around *us* in this country. There is nothing to do and it brings with it an inner emptiness to us all; an unnamed fear, something lurking. Despair. Before we go. You're so very kind. I'll come with you. (*He looks at the door then away, lifts her hair. Beat.*) I don't want to know your name.

104

Blackout. Silence then for about six or seven seconds we hear the unfeasibly loud throm of a giant industrial drill.

Transition. Back up near the dig we are in a barn which has been turned into a sort of hospitality room. At the back is a flat-screen TV which shows the rescue. Owen and Bun are there, as is Fork the Cat. There is a carnival atmosphere and a large crowd over the hill. Waves of country music are carried on the wind and they all but drown out the drill. Bun is bumming his chat with Fork the Cat. Owen is setting up some doc lights in the corner. Ellen stands near them, in her own world. She looks very distraught.

Bun So what I do is this . . .

Ellen comes a little bit closer, wheeling a chequered 'old lady' trolley.

Fork the Cat Are you alright, love?

Ellen (*quiet*) 'I don't know where I'm goin' but I'm goin' to people who love me.'

As she stands looking around her, Fork makes a sign as if to say 'Is she nuts?'

Bun She's puttin' it on. Oh aye, they're all at it. My ma's the same. It's the new deaf.

They both look at her, she starts to move across the stage, then they drop the interest.

Anyway. Every time there's a wedding, you see –

At the word 'wedding' Ellen stops slightly then moves slower. He's got her interest.

– what I like to do is take the cake-cutting knife –

She walks very slowly. As she does we see the pain of this register on her face bit by bit.

– and stick a bit of meat under the silver paper. A gristly oul' bit of sirloin, the best for drippin' blood. Oh ho ho. You should see their faces –

Ellen becomes more crumpled by the second.

– and if we're really lucky it drips on their dress. And then, you should see their faces –

Ellen stops and turns slowly during:

– red on white. Thinkin' it's an omen and all. Oh the marriages I must have blighted.

Even Fork the Cat is horrified.

Fork the Cat You wanna get some therapy, mate. You're very passive aggressive.

Bun What? Well that's rich isn't it, coming from a man who sticks forks in cats.

They both stare at Bun. He only sees Fork the Cat.

Fork the Cat (*handing him a card*) Here. She's great at the oul' healin', puts stones on yer back and ye can get a grant.

Bun What? I don't need healed. I am not a bloody terrorist.

Fork the Cat (*snapping the card back*) Well, you fuckin' terrify me.

Lally arrives as if directed through the door by unseen hands. She is numb, spent, damaged. Immediately on edge at the sight of where she is, she tries to focus and look around.

Lally What's this place? Why am I in this place?

Fork the Cat Don't worry. You're safe. It belongs to a friend of mine.

Lally (*worrying*) Oh really. A friend of *yours*? Many of them, have ye?

Francis (*licking the cream out of an éclair*) You alright, love? Are you hungry at all? Is yer ankles at ye? Do you mebbe need a wee chair?

Lally is almost shaking, still taking in the scene. Bun scowls at her. Fork the Cat stands at the door barring the way while trying to look like he's not there. Ellen stands quietly weeping.

Lally (*to Francis, re: the éclair*) Where did you get that?

The megaphone sparks into life outside. This is the Compère. He has a broad local accent and sounds like a DJ at a wedding.

Compère (*megaphone*) I have just been reliably informed that there's refreshments at the bottom of the hill –

Ellen collapses on the floor with grief.

(*Megaphone.*) – refreshments provided kindly o'course by McTasney's bakery and sundry provisions.

Lally Just check there isn't a razor blade in it.

Francis looks at the éclair. Lally goes over to Fork the Cat. She whispers.

It's sorted. You know I sorted it. I don't need to be in here. The priest has had his publicity.

Fork the Cat That's nice.

Lally What harm would it do me being up there? I sorted it. You said that would be all it took.

Fork the Cat (*kindly, genuinely*) We have been known to lie.

Francis Why don't you just hang on here? They know what they're doing. (*Preening.*) Turns out I am an old school chum, of the main man himself.

Compère (*megaphone*) Please form an orderly queue and use the bins provided.

Owen Don't worry, I'm sure you'll be reunited with him in no time.

Fork the Cat That'll be a thing to watch.

Bun (*knowingly*) That'll be the dogs.

Owen It's probably best that you stay here for your own protection. It's still very volatile out there. This whole mad story has unfolded at such a rate. It's a veritable rollercoaster of a ride.

Compère (*megaphone*) I have just been reliably informed that bins will be provided.

Very wary, Lally stands swaying, her legs about to go. Nobody notices.

Owen I've spent weeks on a reality TV ice dance programme, afraid, yes afraid that my fingers might find their way over the windpipe of a *Cash in the Attic* cunt. Who's suddenly discovered what we all knew, that she can do the splits upside down –

He finally notices Lally's distress. He gets up and gets her a chair during . . .

– but I can honestly say I've managed to almost block out the sheer wretchedness of my life by the distraction of what's happening outside.

Lally sits down carefully. Slight pause.

Francis I could have done that.

Owen Yes you could.

Francis I can look after my wife

Lally I can look after myself.

Owen takes her bandaged hand, she struggles a bit. He stops her. He starts to take off the bandage, gently. Whatever thought is going through Francis' head, it is soon lost.

Owen Where were you? Jesus, darlin', what did you have to do?

Nothing. But she lets him take off the bandage. It's quite intimate. This is the only gentleness in the room. She's now shattered, and it takes everything for her not to break.

Whatever you say, say nothin', right?

Lally Specially to someone like you.

Ellen Everyone's just a cunt.

Francis Mother!

Owen If somebody hurt you, Lally, we can help. Call the authorities. The police.

Everybody onstage laughs a little.

Lally I don't need the authorities. I met the Holy Roman Emperor.

Ellen Decent woman'll do anything to protect her child. That's a sign of decency!

Breaking, Lally starts to laugh.

Bun Look, mate, I can't just hang around all day. Can we just get started, yeah?

Ellen (*distraught*) But sometimes you have to choose. (*Shouts at Bun.*) Who wants you here!

Bun (*pointing at Owen*) Him!

Lally winks at Owen. She looks a bit nuts. Francis goes and puts his hands on her.

Francis She's got me.

Owen Yes she has. Holy God.

Fork the Cat Erm, I'm not here for the view neither. I'm a very busy man.

Owen (*to Lally*) This is to help you.

Lally What is.

Ellen Oh, like a big white knight.

Lally What!

Owen I'm sorry. But I can't walk away from you twice.

Lally What are ye's doing to me now!

Bun As a representative of the local traders and vintners' association and chairman of the board of the county association of turf accountants, did you think I wouldn't have been informed of what the fuck you've been up to?

Lally Oh God.

Bun I have it under good authority that that there fellah there –

Owen It's true.

Ellen (*to Bun*) Don't you even *speak* to my son.

Bun – I have information from my associates in the turf accounting trade that that fellah there has been placing bets –

Lally Francis. You told me you didn't have a *brilliant* bloody idea.

Bun – placin' bets with regularity, since the origin of the *whole* episode. Information which I of course had to pass on to our own local boy Owen here.

Lally You stood and told me you didn't have a *stroke* of fucking genius!

Francis What? I just put a bet on the races. Accumulator kind of a yoke. It's the Derby on Saturday.

Fork the Cat No, I think you'll find it's not.

Compère (*megaphone*) Could the owner of the red Alexis registration number F21 . . .

Owen Which unfortunately only served to confirm the suspicions I already had.

Compère (*megaphone*) . . . Sorry. F22 67Z1 please remove it or it'll be towed away.

Francis twigs. Finally.

Francis But. What. Noh! Don't look at me like *that*. I didn't do a thing to the *child*!

Owen I can't walk away from you again.

Francis I never harmed my chile! Oh sweet Jesus, I would never do a thing like that!

Lally So what are we doing in here!

Francis I'm not some sort of an animal!

Owen I had no option. In the interests of truth and for your privacy and protection, I made the choice to work with local bodies to facilitate an exclusive.

Bun We're going to film the reunion/confession later, privately like, in here.

Francis I just wanted to get some nice things for my wife!

Owen Just as soon as Gavin gets back with the camera. I haven't a fucking clue where he is.

Bun starts to preen himself for the shoot.

Francis I just wanted to buy a few wee . . . We've never had nothin', you know?!

Lally No. What are we doing in *here*? In this barn? Do you know what they used to do here?

Owen looks confused. Fork the Cat starts to get busy.

Fork the Cat You should thank this man as a matter of a fact. Our boy Owen has done yous a favour. You see, I don't know if you know this, but it's something I have workshopped. It seems that within the first few days of a news story breaking, a received view emerges of events, and that is the view to which most of them run-of-the-mill journalists out *there* are gonna conform . . .

Owen, quite understandably, looks at Fork the Cat.

I mean, for fuck's sake, have none of yous no . . . concept of perception?

Fork the Cat takes Francis in a headlock, deadlegs him like a pro and starts to tie him up.

Lally Oh dear Jesus. (*To Owen.*) What have you done?!

Owen What? Wait . . . what are you . . . what the hell is this?

Fork the Cat We're in a continuous period of adjustment, it is imperative that we implement the tools –

Owen Excuse me!

Fork the Cat – to stop puttin' the adjustment in jeopardy and drawin' attention to bein' a cunt.

Lally You . . . don't you know what he is?

Owen What on earth do you think you're going to do?

Fork the Cat Whatever it is, it isn't kneejerk, I can honestly assure you of that.

Owen (*laughing*) They're not going to do anything. Stop being ridiculous!

Fork the Cat You wanted an exclusive. This is how we get one here.

Lally This is where they used to take you before you become an 'X' on a map.

Owen (*laughing*) This is ludicrous.

Fork the Cat As a reluctant representative of the local all-party policing board –

Ellen Stop laughing!

Bun I'd *love* to be on that board.

Fork the Cat – let me rephrase that, I'm not reluctantly a representative, I'm just reluctantly about to fuck you up.

Compère (*megaphone*) Eh . . . we've just had a very serious announcement . . .

Hearing this, Lally gets up.

Owen I think you may have misunderstood what I meant by . . . This is not what I wanted . . . Whatever this is . . .

Lally Wait!

Bun Citizen's arrest.

Fork the Cat (*laughing*) Who are you calling a citizen?

Ellen (*to Owen*) See what you've gone and done?

Bun This is sanctioned by the community. It's co-operation. We took a poll.

Fork the Cat I like to call it tenderising. I promise to leave his face.

Owen What?!

Francis I only done it . . . to buy you nice wee things.

Fork the Cat has hoisted him up and is attaching him to some manacles. There is a gasp from the crowd outside.

Lally?

Lally (*trying to listen*) Shut up!

Owen But. You can't do this. This is barbaric. This isn't what you do now.

Francis Corner sofa to sit on . . . and a trampoline for the kids.

Bun I promise you I have worked with this man on many's an occasion and I have never found him to be anything less than professional.

Francis Lally?

Lally I'm sorry, but please shut up!

She goes to the door. Bun stops her. There is another gasp from outside and another screech from the megaphone. Lally turns out, terrified.

What!

Owen You can't just string a man up in a barn. Not in any civilised land.

Francis (*distraught*) You're nothin' without a trampoline in the new Ireland, you know?

Owen This must be some sort of learnt behaviour. Christ! It's like takin' a step back into the past.

Bun Isn't it amazing how quickly that can happen?

Fork the Cat (*snaps his fingers, vicious*) Really, just like *that*.

Lally Something's happening. Please SHUT UP!

Bun Should he not be upside down?

Owen Look, you don't have to do this. On some level you might think you do, but you have a choice. Need to take a minute to think.

Fork the Cat (*turning and staring at Bun*) What did you just say?

Owen (*frantic*) There is *always* an alternative to violence and murder. We've come so far. It's not ingrained. Think of the future – the . . . the . . . the people, out there. They'd never sanction what you're about to do! Have faith in them. Listen to them as they cry out for peace. Listen as their voices rise up in a unified fucking hymn for peace!

Flash transition. Daly as if on screen. Rahab stands beside him, transfixed by the camera. Lucky Gav is doing the interviewing.

Daly (*with the two puppets up at his face, alternately listening to them and speaking out*) I know. I know. I know. I know. I know. I know. I know! (*To the puppets.*) I warned them, didn't I warn them, but would they listen? (*He removes one of the puppets.*) No. They gave them the inch! (*To the other puppet.*) Did you not hear me say 'inch'? (*Removes the other puppet and then begins to take off the jacket.*) But don't be thinking now that I'm just gonna . . . *stand* here with one hand as long as the other. Because, we are a civilised Ulster now so we are . . . with liaising . . . and hear this, that now that my shift is over and tomorrow is my day off . . . (*Jacket is off, the old Daly is back.*) Heads will be split and skulls will be cracked and I will wash in the blood of the outrage. I will stick my hands in the blood of the outrage. I will have evenin' gloves up to here of the raw hot red blood of what is so alien to civilised me! Because we're like everybody else now, aren't we? And I will get involved, I am inclusive. And modern. And I will show photos of entrails on internet social networking sites. And I will take the eyes out and feast on the innards, knit me a banner of the guts and have online petitions in blood and shit and cyber piss! And I will Photoshop me ripping the baby from her belly and *digitally feasting* on the meconium off its wretched scut head. Because I have never had an original thought in my life. And a life lived in fear is the only decent life to live. And I believe everything I read. And I hear and I see and I'M TOLD. And if I was cloned and all my cloned brains were laid end to end in a room there wouldn't be the brain power to lift a hair on a gnat's arse! But that doesn't mean I'm not valid and I don't have the right, the right by birth, the absolute fucking right . . .

Gav Yes, I think we've enough there.

Daly There! You're doin' it again! Hey you fuck! You bigot! You inciter! It *clearly* says on the BBC that MY OPINION MATTERS!

> *He stands threatening with a bat, a tableau of rage. Rahab stands beside him still staring at the camera, stagestruck.*

Transition. Back to where we were. Lally is still standing looking out, petrified. Owen stares at Fork the Cat and Fork the Cat is livid with Bun.

Compère (*megaphone: a bit pissed off now.*) I told yous *before* to stand *behind* the perimeter fence. Yous are totally hinderin' the dig. Yous can see all you want on the video screens that's been erected!

Lally nearly falls over with relief.

Fork the Cat What did you just say? To me?

Lally I thought he was dead.

Bun I just said would it not be better now, if yer bhoy there was upside down? You know . . . No?

Lally I thought he had fallen down.

Fork the Cat Oh I heard what you said, Mr floury doughballs expert *supervisor*. When I asked you to repeat yourself I was in fact being furious.

Bun I have a right . . .

Owen Lally?

Francis Lally?

Fork the Cat Upside down. Did you read that in a book?

Bun No, I saw it –

Francis I love you.

Fork the Cat In a film? Are we playin' charades?

Bun (*weakly*) – in a . . . I think it was in . . . a play.

Pause. The full flip.

Fork the Cat Oh. (*Furiously cold.*) Well then, of *course*. Fuck me. If it was in one of *them*.

He looks at Bun like he'd like to kill him, then walks off. Something has popped. He begins to rummage around among some stuff at the back wall. There is the sound of boxes being moved and metal objects being disturbed.

Lally I know.

Fork the Cat (*muttering*) 'Make an adjustment', they say. 'Co-operate and fuckin' liaise'. 'Give the *women* a leg up' if 'leg up' is not a sexist *terminality*. Equality this and equality up my hole. And now Mr marzipan fruit ballsack there, thinks he has the right . . .

Lally I thought he was gone.

Francis (*crying*) I know.

Owen Oh.

Ellen Yeah, fuckin' 'Oh'.

Bun I am acting in an advisory capacity.

Owen (*trying to take charge*) Look, you, whatever the fuck your name is, that's enough. You need to just calm down.

Fork the Cat (*stops rummaging*) I am so *fucking tired* of being told to calm down.

Francis Don't tell him to calm down!

Fork the Cat (*starts rummaging again, angrily*) We never hung anyone upside down, for your *information*. FYI! Because if we had hung them upside down we knew there was the strong possibility –

Bun I was tryin' to assist.

Fork the Cat – that the blood rushes to his head, and then he passes out and misses all the craic –

Francis I'm not an evil man.

Fork the Cat – trying to teach him a lesson, you *amateur*, not give him a fucking migraine.

After a brief rummage he appears with a hammer.

I have grown to hate the word 'workshop'. I really, really have . . . In fact the only person who should use the word 'workshop'? Is a fellah with one of these in his hand.

Owen You're not going to do anything with that. There are hundreds of people outside.

Ellen He can do what he likes in here.

Lally He's the co-owner of this barn.

Fork the Cat wheels out a large object covered in a sheet. He places it next to Francis.

Owen I was dealing with democratically elected local government. I was dealing with . . .

Fork the Cat (*to Bun*) Hey, Helen Mirren . . .

He whips off the covering. It is a large industrial mincer. For large industrial amounts of mince.

How do you like my *prop*?

No one laughs . . . they are terrified.

Francis Sweet Jesus. Somebody get me down! His fuckin' therapy hasn't worked.

Fork the Cat Actually we've recently turned a corner, not that *anybody*'s interested.

Nobody moves. Fork the Cat looks at them and turns the handle on the mincer. Some old mince plops out on to the ground. There is a pause. Nobody should know what to say.

(*All thrilled with himself.*) Oops.

Same.

(*Not so thrilled.*) What?

Pause. Shifts about.

Bun Fork the Cat. Mate, in all seriousness. That is a bit –

Fork the Cat What?

Same.

Too much? What? (*Beat.*) What? That? It's a joke.

Bun – very inappropriate.

Fork the Cat It's a joke.

Bun *Some* would say *offensive.*

Fork the Cat No. No. I was trying to . . . I was tryin' to frighten a confession out of cunty there.

Bun And you criticised my sirloin?

Fork the Cat We're not allowed to *do* any of that any more. He (*Owen*) just said that. All I have left is the fear. (*Beat.*) It's just a joke. A practical *jape.* A gag. Involving fear.

Pause.

(*Pointing at the mince.*) That's not real *person.* That's from Tesco's skip.

Owen I . . . I really need to get the fuck out of here.

Bun You should maybe get yer sponsor on the phone.

Owen I need to get some air.

Fork the Cat looks very agitated. He turns to Owen.

Fork the Cat You're not about to misrepresent me in the press, are you? I'm under enough pressure as it is.

Bun Just hang on for a second there, Owen. The fellah was *obviously* havin' a joke. Simply tryin' his level best to *gently intimidate* a confession.

Fork the Cat I can't do actual damage any more. So you'll not go round sayin' I do.

Owen (*nearly in tears*) How can you even . . . ? How is that ever a joke?

Lally It's all just a big joke now.

Fork the Cat Postmodernist conflict humour?

Pause.

More than enough time has passed since the cessation of violence to allow for a humorous discourse on atrocity.

Owen No it hasn't! Oh dear God, it hasn't.

Fork the Cat Fuck you. Fuck. You.

Owen looks at the mince.

(*Looking shifty.*) That's a prop.

Pause.

Just a prop.

They all stare at it.

It's about perception, Owen. Stop looking at the prop!

Owen You people are . . . this is way too much for me.

Lally Times of adjustment are hard.

Bun So the big exclusive's out the winda?

Owen No. Yes. God, Jesus. Yes! I've . . . I have no wish for one of those.

Ellen turns and looks at him, like she's just woken up.

Owen I can't *believe* any of you. No. I don't want an exclusive. You're all too fucking exclusive. This is even worse than before. You need to just say . . . just say I've changed my mind about any of that.

Ellen Your mind?

Fork the Cat (*quietly*) Not because of me.

Lally Now can you let my husband down?

Fork the Cat Shit.

Owen I got it wrong. I'm sorry. Sometimes. Sometimes we get it *very* wrong.

Ellen Your mind?

Owen There's . . . there's no story here. There's nothing. I just want to go home. Lally, take your boy and run far from here. I won't write a fucking word.

Lally (*calmly, to Fork the Cat*) Could I have my husband back please?

Ellen Oh Jesus. Oh Jesus, help me please.

A very dangerously sheepish Fork the Cat lets Francis down. Owen looks at Lally.

Owen I'm sorry. I must have a different reference point. I don't know what the rules are any more.

Ellen Oh Jesus.

Fork the Cat Well, *this* certainly isn't awkward.

Fork the Cat heads back to the door and relieves Bun. Bun then spots Ellen.

Bun High, missus. What's wrong with you? You're lookin' very white.

Compère (*megaphone*) Ladies and gentlemen we have just had word from the fire brigade . . .

All stop except Bun and Ellen.

Bun As white as royal icing. As white as a wedding cake.

Transition. Lighting change to earlier on the side of the hill. The drill fades to a dull noise. Digger Barnes stands wiping sweat out of his eyes. He is demolishing bits from a tier of a wedding cake. He cuts them with a large knife wrapped in silver paper. Ellen comes on. She stands watching him.

Barnes (*catches her looking at him*) Jesus. How long have you been there? Gimme a heart . . . What are ye, the grey assassin?

Ellen Sure I'm no threat, am I? Big strong fellah like you.

She mosies over. He reluctantly lets her. She tries to pretend to be a passer-by.

So what's goin' on with the scuts on the hill? (*Beat, laugh.*) I heard the craic with the relocate . . .

Barnes I know who you are.

Ellen Oh.

Barnes Aye. What do you wanna know?

Ellen What?

Barnes How long it'll take?

Ellen Why would I wanna know that?

Barnes Your precious son did.

Ellen Never you mind him! Oh Jesus, what did he say?

Barnes He asked me what time we'd get him out, as if it's an exact science, the thick.

Ellen Oh aye, the thick. The thick!

Barnes Do you know what we used to call him at school, we'd call him –

Ellen His oul' da used to call him that too. And I'd say

123

noh, he's not. And the fights we'd have over it. Fights. But you're right . . .

Pause.

He is. How's that cake?

Barnes I suppose *you* want a bit.

Ellen You lose the taste for fancy things when all that's give ye's gristle.

Barnes Whatever. Are you OK?

Ellen He's my son. And I only have the one. You see? You see?

Barnes Missus, look, I've enough on my plate, could you just maybe fuck away off?

Pause. Ellen pulls herself together.

Ellen I'd say it'll be not long at all till you're level with the wee cub.

Barnes No, missus, you don't go level. You see what you have to do is –

Ellen – reach over and grab him and Bob and Fanny's the oul' uncle and aunt.

Barnes You don't do that. If you would just listen –

Ellen Your funeral.

Barnes What?

Ellen Far be it from a little old lady to question yer smart expertise but exactly how much oxygen do you think you have to play with down there?

Pause.

Barnes No. That's . . . they said . . .

Ellen Who said?

Barnes ALL OF THEM! EVERYBODY. I have friends in the media.

Ellen (*laughs*) Well mebbe they can stop ye gettin' strung up.

Barnes Whose gonna string me up?

Ellen Round here? You in the public eye and puttin' workmen down there in an oul' underneath and horizontal fashion. Workmen wi' wives and childer and it takin' way, way longer than it should?

Barnes Oh.

Ellen And them same workmen runnin' out of air and gaspin' for breath, not to mention the child . . . and *therego* you get strung up because of listenin' to the media and other assorted eejits about goin' underneath.

Pause. Ellen shrugs. Barnes looks petrified.

Barnes They actually said they wanted it to take longer. I'm not tellin' no lie! How could I have known then that they were settin' me up?

Pause.

They said they were interested in me; get me an agent! What am I gonna do?

Ellen Well you can either listen to . . . devious *manipulative* people or listen to your own expertise.

Barnes I *was* gonna go level.

Ellen What? Well, there you are. You know best, not them.

Barnes The scuts!

Ellen So how now, should it go? Havin' reconsidered. After all, you're the expert.

Barnes We go level with him, reach out and grab him. Get him up as quick as –

Ellen Sounds much more feasible.

Barnes There might be a bit of a break or dislocation but nothin' that won't heal.

Pause.

But what if he falls?

Pause.

Ellen If he falls –

Pause.

– that's not down to you. But if he suffocates . . . they all suffocate from fannyin' around underneath? How's that gonna look?

Barnes Oh God, you're right. I'm not gonna listen to nobody!

Ellen Workmen dead cos of you. Whole thing down to you.

Barnes I'm just an ordinary fellah. I'm just too trusting. All them coconut jokes –

Ellen Happen to anyone.

Barnes I need to think for myself. Thank you. You're right. That was close.

Ellen Me. Why? What was it I done, son?

Barnes I would never have had myself down for someone so easily manipulated, you know?

Ellen cuts a slice of the wedding cake with the knife and looks at it, then gently hands it to him. She watches as he stuffs the cake into his mouth, a terrible look on her indeed.

Transition. Back in the barn. The noise of the crowd gets louder like an evaporation in reverse. Lally looks at Owen during . . .

Compère (*megaphone*) Now just everybody calm down. We need quiet now. The fire brigade has just told us. They're almost level . . . the little one is practically in reach.

Lally stays looking at Owen, her face changes, a horror dawning.

Lally He said 'level'.

Compère (*megaphone*) We're lowering down a camera. If you look at the monitors like I said we are level with the little one now.

Lally He just said 'level' again.

Owen turns to Bun, accusatory. Bun shrugs, nothing to do with him. Then he turns to Ellen.

Compère (*megaphone*) You should be able to see the first pictures of the boy.

On the TV we can just make out the grainy image of a child. It's like a scan.

Lally Nobody must have listened.

Compère (*megaphone*) You can just see. I can just see . . . What's that? Is that an arm?

Lally After all that, they're just grabbing in the dark.

Ellen tries to get away from Bun. He follows, he's not letting her away.

They haven't put anything there. A foundation. A brace . . .

Compère (*megaphone*) I don't know about you, but I don't think I've seen such emotion.

Lally (*going over to Owen*) Help me. I'll give you anything you want.

Owen (*walking away*) I don't know the rules.

Lally I'll tell you what they are.

His phone rings.

Owen (*avoiding her, on the phone*) What. Hello?

Compère (*megaphone*) It is. I think it's an arm. Is it moving? Can we see? It's very dark down there, isn't it?

Lally turns to the TV.

(*Megaphone.*) The crowd is completely silent . . .

Owen (*on the phone*) Yes . . . yes . . . oh . . . right, I see.

Compère (*megaphone*) All the local people gathered together. United. In hope.

Owen (*on the phone*) What are you saying?

Compère (*megaphone*) Turning a situation of horror –

Lally Oh my wee pet.

Bun (*going right up behind Ellen, smiling*) Don't you worry. I'm a very patient man. Whatever you done, it can wait. For now anyway, wha?

Owen (*on the phone*) What age? What sex? What nationality?

Compère (*megaphone*) – into one of community . . . uh . . . unity.

Lally Oh the pain of it. Wee bones. Break like kindling. Let him not fall back.

Owen (*on the phone*) Book it immediately. I don't care about first class.

He hangs up and starts to put his gear away.

Bun All this can keep till later. Till everyone's gone away.

He pats her on the shoulder.

Then you can give me the lowdown. And all of us round here will figure out what to do.

He walks away and pulls up a chair and sits down at the TV like it's a movie. Ellen stands. Motionless.

Compère (*megaphone*) The whole country is holding its breath. And it's so difficult to see. But is that . . . is that . . .

Francis (*looking at the TV*) Look, look. Is that his . . . ? What's that?

Lally After all that.

Ellen takes her trolley and quietly wheels it over behind Bun. She watches the TV too.

Compère (*megaphone, dropping to a whisper*) The crowd here united in their support.

Bun (*to Owen*) You away? They're just about to get him out.

Lally No.

Compère (*megaphone*) Never giving up for a second. And now the child within reach.

Owen Yes . . . ahm . . . that was a call. I have to get myself on a flight . . . I'm sorry, no alternative . . .

Compère (*megaphone*) These pictures are amazing . . .

Lally Be gentle with my baby.

Compère (*megaphone*) Just a millimetre more and . . . that's it.

Owen I'm afraid a story's broken. In Greece. There's a child . . . missing . . . a little girl.

Compère (*megaphone*) The world holds its breath and watches us.

Owen From Surrey . . .

Lally That's his skin.

Owen I need to go there right away. You see within the first few days of a story breaking, a received . . .

No one's listening. He goes to leave. Fork the Cat watches him. They lock eyes. Lally can't look any more. She walks to the middle of the stage. Looks out. Owen is gone.

Francis Is that? Lally? Is that . . .

Compère (*megaphone*) You could hear a global pin drop.

Suddenly there is the distant noise of hundreds of mobile phones ringing at once.

(*Megaphone.*) Wait . . . what the fuck? What the hell is goin' on?

The noise of feet, car doors slamming.

Francis What? What's that noise? What's happening? What's . . . what's going on?

Compère (*megaphone*) People seem to be moving away.

Helicopters taking off in the distance. The noise is excruciating. Lights flash through the windows and cracks of the barn.

Compère (*megaphone*) Why is the crowd . . . reporters . . . the press . . . moving away?

Lally First flight to Greece would be my best bet.

The TV switches over to a studio. With a 'breaking news' flash. 'IN GREECE: A CHILD MISSING . . . FROM SURREY'. Francis tries to get their story back. He can't.

It's gone.

Compère (*megaphone*) Dirt seems to be falling. Jesus, will you stop!

Bun (*laughing*) Well of course, of course! Sure you could have seen that comin' a mile off, couldn't you?

Ellen looks at him sitting there laughing. She then takes out the cake knife. She expertly slits his throat. He falls to the floor silently. Nobody notices.

Compère (*megaphone*) Please think of what you're doing! The child . . . think of him, please.

Pause.

(*Megaphone.*) Oh this is bad. People are in tears. Nothing that young could survive this. Too fragile. Too many obstacles. Think of what you're doing in the name of Christ . . . this is very delicate.

The TV crackles and fizzes. It starts to glare white and bright noise.

(*Megaphone.*) Get out of the way, I can't see. Is that? I can't see but I think it is. Fuck me. I think I see his hand. Graspin'. I think I see, I can see him holdin' on for dear life. I think I see blood. But it's not on him. He's causing it. Drawing it from his rescuer. Wee young thing knotting fingers round anything they can find. Sharp nails digging in. Clambering for a way up. Up and out. Well. (*Beat.*) Now.

Pause. Nobody moves. Absolute stillness. Lally clenches her fists.

(*Megaphone.*) Do you think something that tiny? Jesus, it's almost rabid. Locked on. Is it possible? Despite everything? I'm not at all sure . . . get out of the way!

Same.

(*Megaphone.*) Is that something behind him? Something at his back? Is that an eye? Teeth? Something dark, making him want to move. It would make me want to move. Forward. Everything's falling backwards but he seems to be climbing now. Up and away from . . . what is that? Do you think he can? Is there a glimmer of hope? Fucked if I know. You have the right to reply.

Pause.

(*Megaphone.*) Is there mebbe hope? Fuck. Have we that? Mebbe? Fuck.

Start fade.

(*Megaphone.*) To hold on? For now even?

Lally Yes.

Compère (*megaphone*) To get away from whatever that is? Down there? Back there. Whatever that is? Wha?

Pause.

(*Megaphone.*) Is there hope? Do you think?

Pause.

(*Megaphone.*) To hold on?

Black except for TV.

Black. End of play.